EMERALD
& TANZANITE
BUYING GUIDE

Text & Photographs
by
Renée Newman

International Jewelry Publications

Los Angeles

This publication is designed to provide information in regard to the subject matter covered. It is sold with the understanding that the publisher and author are not engaged in rendering legal, financial, or other professional services. If legal or other expert assistance is required, the services of a competent professional should be sought. International Jewelry Publications and the author shall have neither liability nor responsibility to any person or entity with respect to any loss or damage caused or alleged to be caused directly or indirectly by the information contained in this book. All inquiries should be directed to:

International Jewelry Publications
P.O. Box 13384
Los Angeles, CA 90013-0384 USA

(Inquiries should be accompanied by a self-addressed, stamped envelope).

Printed in Singapore

Library of Congress Cataloging in Publication Data

Newman, Renée.
     The emerald & tanzanite buying guide / text & photographs by Renée Newman.
          p.   cm.
     Includes bibliographical references and index.
     ISBN 0-929975-23-5 : $19.95
     1. Emeralds--Purchasing. 2. Zoisite--Purchasing.
I. Title
TS755.E5N48   1995
553.8'6'0297--dc20   95-8606
                                                CIP

Cover photographs:

Left photo: Diamond necklace pendant set with a 13.37-ct pear shape emerald. Photo and necklace courtesy Harry Winston Inc., New York City.

Right photo: Diamond necklace pendant set with a 96.42-ct tanzanite. Photo and necklace courtesy Tiffany & Co.

Contents

Contents

Preface

Why wouldn't an emerald dealer want to teach customers how to evaluate emeralds?

I asked myself this question while escorting a group of tourists around South America. We were visiting an emerald firm in Bogotá, Colombia. The manager there showed us a film about the mining, cutting and marketing of emeralds. Afterwards we browsed in a showroom of high-class jewelry. But no one in the company ever told us how to evaluate emerald quality. One passenger commented, "Why should I spend thousands of dollars for an emerald ring in Colombia when I can buy one at my local discount store for a couple hundred?"

I became interested in gems while working as a full-time tour director in South America, Asia and the South Pacific. We often visited gem firms like the one in Colombia, and my passengers wanted to know what to look for when buying colored stones. I went to the library to find the answer. Although there were books on gem identification, mining, synthesis, history, lore and world sources, I couldn't find information on how to judge the quality of colored gems.

When I heard about a five-day colored-stone grading course at the GIA (Gemological Institute of America), I decided to enroll. Janice Mack was the instructor and Susan Johnson, her assistant. In one week at the GIA, I learned more about evaluating colored gems than in five years of exposure to them while traveling abroad. The enthusiasm and dedication of the instructors inspired me to sign up for the gemology program at the GIA. Two years later, I obtained a GIA GG diploma and began work as a gemologist for a wholesale firm in downtown Los Angeles. I wanted practical experience that would help me write consumer guides to buying gems and jewelry.

My books have been well-received by many jewelers. A few, however, have told me my books could ruin their business, and they've given reasons why they don't want to teach customers how to evaluate gems. Since consumer education is an important and controversial topic, I've decided to list some of their reasons and comment on them.

9

♦ *If customers learn about quality differences, they'll only want the best. Since they won't be able to afford it, they'll end up buying nothing.*

Informed consumers learn to make choices that fit their budget. Diamond education has not kept people from buying flawed, yellowish diamonds. To save money, people will buy lower quality goods. They just want to know what they are getting for their money.

♦ *If I teach customers how to compare prices, they won't buy my jewelry.*

Jewelers with over-priced goods are probably right about this. However, in the long run, it's more productive to charge fair prices than to hide information from the public. Informed customers are willing to spend more money on good jewelry because they understand why it is worth more. People who are uninformed tend to shop for the lowest price in town without any regard to quality differences.

♦ *My customers are only interested in price and style. They could care less about quality.*

Jewelers who never talk quality tend to drive away customers interested in quality. Jewelers who educate their customers attract a clientele that appreciates fine jewelry.

♦ *A little knowledge is a dangerous thing. Customers who learn about quality think they know it all and don't accept any advice.*

When it comes to buying gems, the more knowledgeable consumers are, the more likely they are to make a wise choice. Well-educated customers understand the complexities of evaluating and identifying gems. After people read my books, they realize the importance of seeking professional guidance.

♦ *Gems should be romanced, not analyzed.*

Stories about the history and lore of gems do not teach us how to appreciate their beauty. For this, we must learn to analyze their quality features. The fact that Cleopatra and Elizabeth Taylor have worn emeralds is of little importance to most gem buyers. They're more interested in knowing if a stone looks good and if it's worth the price.

♦ *We hired a gemologist who tried to teach customers how to judge quality. She was the worst salesperson this store ever had.*

It's true that a gemologist without selling skills can turn out to be a poor salesperson. However, a super-seller without product knowledge can be equally unsuccessful. Even though most customers don't want a technical dissertation on quality analysis, they do appreciate salespeople who can explain price differences and provide clear, accurate answers to their questions. A number of stores have told me they often have their gemologist(s) close the sales of high-ticket items. They've found that customers respond better to knowledgeable salespeople.

During my time as a tour director, I noticed, too, that the most effective salespeople were those who could explain quality. Most of the pearl sellers I knew in the Orient would show my passengers how differences in color, luster, shape, and blemish quality affected their price. A high percentage of my tour members ended up buying pearls, and it was not uncommon for them to spend over $1000 on a purchase. They appreciated that the salespeople wanted to help them buy intelligently.

The majority of the emerald sellers I met while tour directing tended to avoid the subject of quality. Very few of my passengers bought emerald jewelry, and the purchases were small except in one case. A store owner in India gained the respect of one of my passengers by candidly discussing his emeralds with her. She ended up buying two stones for $4000. She had a prior knowledge of emeralds, so she felt comfortable that she was getting a good buy.

You won't find much in my books about the mining, history and lore of gems. My goal has been to give consumers the kind of information my passengers and I were looking for--practical guidelines on evaluating and selecting gems and jewelry. In order to provide adequate depth, I've focused on just one or two gems in each book.

Several people have asked me to do a book on tanzanite, a violetish-blue stone discovered in Tanzania in the 1960's. A few independent jewelers have told me it's their best selling colored stone. There have been a lot of requests, too, for a book on judging emerald quality. I have decided to combine information on the two stones into one book. By comparing emerald and tanzanite in the same book, you end up with a better understanding of each stone. Both of these stones can be a major investment, and you can't afford to make the wrong choice or buy from an unreliable person. Use this book along with the advice of your jeweler to select the emeralds or tanzanite that will suit both your pocketbook and your needs.

Acknowledgments

I would like to express my appreciation to the following people for their contribution to the *Emerald & Tanzanite Buying Guide*:

Ernie and Regina Goldberger of the Josam Diamond Trading Corporation. This book could never have been written without the experience and knowledge I gained from working with them. Some of the stones pictured in this book are or were part of their collection.

The American Gemological Laboratories and the Gemological Institute of America. They have contributed diagrams and information.

Pete Flusser, Carrie Ginsberg, Louise Harris, Alan Hodgkinson, Danny Levy, Peter Malnekoff, Cynthia Marcusson, Howard Rubin, Sindi Schloss, Leo Schmied, Maurice Shire, Robert Shire and Abe Suleman. They have made valuable suggestions, corrections, and comments regarding the portions of the book they examined. They are not responsible for any possible errors, nor do they necessarily endorse the material contained in this book.

Pete & Bobbi Flusser, Carrie Ginsberg Fine Gems, Grogan & Co., Danny & Ronny Levy Fine Gems, Eva Kemper, Overland Gems, Inc., Theresa Potts and Marge Vaughn. Their stones have been used for some of the photographs.

Asian Institute of Gemological Sciences, Maurice Badler Fine Jewelry, Grieger's Inc., Alan Hodgkinson, Cynthia Renée Co., Howard Rubin, Tiffany & Co., Harold & Erica Van Pelt and Harry Winston Inc. Photos or diagrams from them have been reproduced in this book.

Ian & Amy Itescu, Donald Nelson and Avery Osborne, They have provided technical assistance.

Patricia S. Esparza. She has spent hours carefully editing the *Emerald & Tanzanite Buying Guide*. Thanks to her, this book is easier for consumers to read and understand.

My sincere thanks to all of these contributors for their kindness and help.

Suppliers of Jewelry & Stones for Photographs

Cover Photos:

Emerald pendant: Harry Winston, Inc., New York, NY
Tanzanite pendant: Tiffany & Co.

Chapter 4

Fig. 4.3   Harry Winston Inc., New York, NY
Fig. 4.4   Cynthia Renée Co., Fallbrook, CA
Fig. 4.8   Harry Winston Inc., New York, NY
Fig. 4.9   Carrie G. & Co. (Carrie Ginsberg Fine Gems), Los Angeles, CA
Fig. 4.13   Harry Winston Inc., New York, NY
Fig. 4.14   Tiffany & Co.
Fig. 4.15   Maurice Badler Fine Jewelry, New York, NY
Fig. 4.16   Grogan & Co., Boston, MA
Fig. 4.17   Harry Winston Inc., New York, NY

Chapter 5

Fig. 5.1   Harry Winston Inc., New York, NY
Figs. 5.2 to 5.4   Danny & Ronny Levy Fine Gems, Los Angeles, CA

Chapter 6

Figs. 6.6 to 6.10   Danny & Ronny Levy Fine Gems, Los Angeles, CA
Figs. 6.19 & 6.20   Carrie G. & Co., Los Angeles, CA

Chapter 7

Figs. 7.1 to 7.6   Carrie G. & Co., Los Angeles, CA
Figs. 7.7 & 7.8   Cynthia Renée Co., Fallbrook, CA
Fig. 7.9   Carrie G. & Co., Los Angeles, Ca
Fig. 7.10   Cynthia Renée Co., Fallbrook, CA

Chapter 8

Figs. 8.3 to 8.5 Carrie G. & Co., Los Angeles, CA
Fig. 8.6 Cynthia, Renée Co., Fallbrook, CA
Figs. 8.7 & 8.8 Overland Gems, Inc., Los Angeles, CA

Chapter 9

Fig. 9.1 Overland Gems, Inc., Los Angeles, CA
Fig. 9.2 Carrie G & Co., Los Angeles, CA
Figs. 9.3 & 9.4 AIGS (Asian Institute of Gemological Sciences), Bangkok, Thailand

Chapter 11

Fig. 11.6 & 11.7 Alan Hodgkinson, Portencross by West Kilbride, Ayrshire, Scotland

1

Why Read a Whole Book Just to Buy an Emerald or Tanzanite?

Elaine was vacationing in Rio de Janeiro and wanted to buy a quality emerald. There was a large jewelry store near her hotel which appeared to have a good selection. She told a salesperson there what she was looking for and he brought out a box with loose emeralds. One deep green stone really caught her eye, but it didn't seem to be very clear. To reassure Elaine, the salesperson told her, "Emeralds have internal features called 'gardens' which do not devalue the stone. In fact, the bigger the 'garden' the better the stone. The 'foliage' gives emeralds a beauty and mystery not possible in eye-clean gems."

Elaine liked the color of the stone, so she went ahead and bought it for $1200. When she took it to her jeweler to have it set in a ring, he told her she'd paid a fair price, but due to its low clarity, it was a below-average emerald. He went on to say that though little "gardens" are normal, good emeralds should not contain big "jungles." As the jeweler examined the stone more closely, he noticed some large fractures which had been filled with epoxy. He then told Elaine that she would be better off wearing the stone in a pendant, where it would be less susceptible to breakage. Elaine wished she had bought a different stone, even if it had cost more. She was mad that the salesperson had not pointed out the large cracks and told her that they had been filled with epoxy.

Charlene had never heard of tanzanite before until she saw some at a going-out-of-business sale. She spotted a unique pear-shape pendant that had been marked down to $400 from $1000. Charlene loved bargains, and since the lilac color of the tanzanite looked good on her, she bought the pendant.

A month later, she was browsing in another jewelry store when she noticed several tanzanite pieces. The stones had more brilliance and sparkle than hers. Charlene happened to be wearing her new pendant and asked the jeweler why her tanzanite looked inferior. He explained to her that it had been cut too shallow. As a result, there was a window through her stone which did not let light and color reflect back to the eye. After seeing what a difference a good cut could make, Charlene regretted her purchase. This was one bargain she wished she had passed up.

While at a flea market, Reuben noticed an attractive ring set with a cluster of emeralds. His girlfriend, Annemarie, was about to have a birthday and her favorite color was green. Figuring the ring would make an ideal gift, Reuben bought it. Annemarie, was really impressed when she opened her present. A few months later, it looked dirty so she let soak in a cleaning solution. Afterwards, she noticed that three of the emeralds had lost most of their color. Reuben was embarrassed when he saw the ring. He didn't remember which vendor had sold him the ring, and he no longer had the sales receipt.

Suppose Elaine had had a book that explained how to examine emeralds and evaluate their clarity. This could have helped her select a better quality emerald.

Suppose Charlene had had a book which showed how cut can affect the beauty of a stone. It would have helped her avoid making a poor buy.

Suppose Reuben had had a book which explained how low-grade emeralds are sometimes filled with colored oil to make them look greener and that they therefore require different cleaning procedures than other gems. He could have either advised Annemarie about proper care or else have purchased another ring elsewhere.

If you glance at the table of contents of the *Emerald & Tanzanite Buying Guide,* you'll notice a wide range of subjects relevant to buying emeralds and tanzanites. There is no way a brochure could cover these subjects adequately. Likewise, it would be impossible for jewelers to discuss thoroughly the grading, identification, pricing, and enhancement of colored stones during a brief visit to their store. It would be better to first learn some fundamental information by reading this book. Jewelers can show you how to apply your new-found knowledge when selecting a stone, and they can help you find what you want.

A knowledge of gems and jewelry will make it easier for you to select a good jeweler. You will learn far more about jewelers by examining their merchandise and discussing it with them than by asking questions such as "How long have you been in business?" "Where were you trained?" "What trade organizations do you belong to?" The answers can be fabricated, and they aren't always a true indication of the jeweler's knowledge, skill or ethics. Therefore, it's important for *you* to be informed about gems. A book on judging gem quality not only helps you select jewelry and gems, it also helps you find a good jeweler.

What This Book Is Not

♦ It's not a guide to making a fortune on emeralds and tanzanites. Nobody can guarantee that these stones will increase in value and that they can be resold for more than their retail cost. However, understanding the value concepts discussed in this book can increase your chances of finding good buys on emeralds and tanzanites.

♦ It's not a ten-minute guide to appraising emerald and tanzanite. There's a lot to learn before being able to accurately compare these stones for value. That's why a book is needed on the subject. The *Emerald & Tanzanite Buying Guide* is just an introduction, but it does have enough information to give laypeople a good background for understanding price differences.

♦ It's not a scientific treatise on the chemistry, crystallography and geological distribution of emerald and tanzanite. The material in this book, however, is based on technical research; the appendix lists the physical and optical properties of these stones to help you identify them. Technical terms needed for buying or grading colored stones are explained in everyday language.

♦ It's not a discussion about the mining and prospecting of emerald and tanzanite. You don't need to know how to mine a gem to buy one. If you're interested in good references on gem mining and sources, some are listed in the bibliography.

♦ It's not a substitute for examining actual stones. Photographs do not accurately reproduce color, nor do they show the three-dimensional nature of gemstones very well. Concepts such as brilliancy and transparency are best understood when looking at real stones.

What This Book Is

♦ A guide to evaluating the quality of emeralds and tanzanites.

♦ An aid to avoiding fraud with tips on detecting imitations, synthetics and treatments.

♦ A handy reference on emeralds and tanzanites for laypeople and professionals.

♦ A collection of practical tips on choosing and caring for emerald and tanzanite jewelry.

♦ A challenge to view emeralds and tanzanites through the eyes of gemologists and gem dealers.

How to Use This Book

The *Emerald and Tanzanite Buying Guide* is not meant to be read like a murder mystery or a romance novel. If you're new to the study of gems, you may find this book overwhelming at first. So start by looking at the pictures and by reading Chapter 2 (Curious Facts about Emerald & Tanzanite), Chapter 13 (Finding a Good Buy), and the Table of Contents. Then learn the basic terminology in Chapter 4 and continue slowly, perhaps a chapter at a time.

Skip over any sections that don't interest you or that are too complicated. This book has far more information than the average person will care to learn. That's because it's also designed to be a reference. When questions arise about emeralds and tanzanites, you can avoid lengthy research by having the answers right at your fingertips.

To get the most out of the *Emerald & Tanzanite Buying Guide*, you should try to actively use what you learn. Buy or borrow a loupe (jeweler's magnifying glass) and start examining any jewelry you might have at home. Take the quizzes you'll find at the end of the book. Look around in jewelry stores and ask the professionals there to show you different qualities and varieties of emeralds and tanzanites. If you have appraisals or grading reports, study them carefully. If there's something you don't understand, ask for an explanation.

Shopping for emeralds and tanzanites should not be a chore. It should be fun. There is no fun, though, in worrying about being deceived or in buying a stone that turns out to be a poor choice. Use this book to gain the knowledge, confidence and independence you need to select the stones that are best for you. Buying gemstones represents a significant investment of time and money. Let the *Emerald & Tanzanite Buying Guide* help make this investment a pleasurable and rewarding experience.

2

Curious Facts about Emerald & Tanzanite

If Cleopatra were alive today, she'd be amazed at how green and vibrant an emerald can be. None of her emeralds were faceted to bring out their brilliance and sparkle. Most were mottled and heavily flawed. Their color tended to be either pale or drab. Nevertheless, these emeralds were regal jewels.

The first known emerald mines were in Egypt. They operated from around 330 BC into the 1700's. Some unconfirmed reports indicate Egyptian deposits might have been exploited as early as 3500 BC. Egypt was the only significant source of emeralds for Asia and Europe until the 1500's, when the Spanish invaded the Americas.

Up to that time, it was unknown to the outside world that various Indian tribes in Central and South America had been using extraordinary emeralds in ornaments and ceremonial objects. These emeralds, which originated from what is now Colombia, were far larger, more transparent, and much greener than those mined in Egypt. During the 16th century, vast quantities of Colombian emeralds entered the European market. The emeralds then made their way to Persia and India and became part of the treasuries of Indian Moguls and Arabian sheiks. Because of the scarcity of green forests and fields in their countries, Muslims have long cherished the color green. In fact, it is the holy color of Islam.

Europeans have also prized emeralds for their color. In the 1st century AD, Roman Scholar Pliny the Elder wrote in his encyclopedic *Natural History*:

Indeed, no stone has a color that is more delightful to the eye, for whereas the sight fixes itself with avidity upon the green grass and foliage of the trees, we have all the more pleasure in looking upon the emerald, there being no green in existence more intense than this. And then, besides, of all the precious stones, this is the only one that feeds the sight without satiating it... If the sight has been wearied or dimmed by intensively looking on any other subject, it is refreshed and restored by gazing at this stone. And lapidaries who cut and engrave fine gems know this well, for they have no better method of restoring their eyes than by looking at the emerald, its soft, green color comforting and removing their weariness and lassitude.

The therapeutic effects of green are even recognized today. The use of the standard "hospital green" is based on the ability of green to induce a sense of calm and rest. In China, people working in fine embroidery factories are encouraged to often glance at green plants and trees to help maintain their eyesight.

Emeralds were also considered to have healing powers when worn. They supposedly cured malaria, cholera and dysentery. They prevented infertility, stillbirths, epileptic seizures, insomnia and pimples--they even served as an antidote against poisons and snakebites.

Additional virtues have been ascribed to the emerald. According to legend, it could sharpen the wits, quicken the intelligence and strengthen the memory. When placed under the tongue, it would help people predict future events. If worn as a birthstone, it would bring good luck and happiness. This belief is alluded to in the following verse from George Kunz's *The Curious Lore of Precious Stones* (p. 328):

Who first beholds the light of day
In spring's sweet flow'ry month of May,
And wears an emerald all her life,
Shall be a loved and happy wife.

It's appropriate that emerald was chosen as the birthstone for the month of May. Its color symbolizes the beauty and promise of nature in the spring of each year.

The rich history of the emerald combined with its beauty and rarity have made it a gem of immense value. In very fine qualities, emeralds can retail for over $20,000 a carat. By comparison, a top grade tanzanite might retail for $1000 a carat. A fine amethyst could sell for $50 a carat. Emeralds have always been treasured for the allure of their intense green color.

An Informal Message from the Tanzanite Family

The price of emerald was just compared to that of tanzanite, and you may have wondered, "What's tanzanite?" Since some of you may have never heard of us before, we tanzanites would like to introduce ourselves. We're a gem that was discovered in the 1960s in the foothills of Africa's Mt. Kilimanjaro, and we come in a variety of shades of blue, violet and purple. Our family name is **zoisite**, but we prefer to be called by our personal name **tanzanite**, the name given to us by Tiffany & Company in honor of our homeland, Tanzania. "Tanzanite" sounds more exotic and appealing than "blue zoisite."

Some of you might be questioning why an obscure gem like tanzanite would be featured in a book about a stone as distinguished as the emerald. We may be a newcomer but we're not without stature. You'll find us in showcases alongside rubies, sapphires, and emeralds. Just have a look at our lush blue and purple colors and you'll see why we've become a big seller.

We have a few things in common with emeralds. We both are from large families with members of various colors. Emeralds are the green variety of the mineral species **beryl** which includes aquamarine. Other beryls are yellow, orange, pink, reddish or colorless. Zoisites are also found in these colors as well as green. Once in a while, beryl and zoisite are cut as cat's-eye stones.

Emeralds and tanzanites are both rare, especially compared to diamonds, which are mined a lot more extensively. The highest percentage of emeralds originate from Colombia. Brazil and Zambia are also major sources of emerald. Tanzania is the sole commercial producer of tanzanite.

We tanzanites are humbled by the emerald. You won't find us in any ceremonial artifacts, royal crown jewels or monuments of ancient civilizations. No mystical powers have been bestowed upon us. No astrological significance has been ascribed to us. No poems or legends about us have been passed on through the ages. Cleopatra was never adorned with tanzanites. But this has not kept us from becoming one of the most popular gems on the market.

We have traits which set us apart from other gems such as emeralds. When you look at us from one angle we may appear blue, but from another angle we will be purple. What's more, we can look one color indoors and another outdoors. Sometimes as you examine us, you will see three colors at once. Along with blue and purple, there may be flashes of red, green, yellow, orange, or brown. We're probably the most difficult transparent gem there is to match. That's because we each have distinctive combinations of color. Our high transparency adds to our beauty. Cutters like to facet us with creative patterns that highlight our brilliance and sparkle.

Once you get to know us, you'll fall in love with us. You may even want to adopt us as your alternate birthstone. So if you haven't had a chance to meet us yet, head on over to your local jeweler and ask to see some tanzanite. You'll be in for a real treat.

3

Carat Weight

The term "carat" originated in ancient times when gemstones were weighed against the carob bean. Each bean weighed about one carat. Gem traders were aware, though, that the weights varied slightly. This made it advantageous for them to own both "buying" beans and "selling" beans.

In 1913, carat weight was standardized internationally and adapted to the metric system, with one carat equalling 1/5 of a gram. The term "carat" sounds more impressive and is easier to use than fractions of grams. Consequently, it is the preferred unit of weight for gemstones.

The weight of small stones is frequently expressed in **points**, with one point equaling 0.01 carats. For example, five points is the same as five one-hundredths of a carat. Contrary to what is sometimes assumed, jewelers do not use "point" to refer to the number of facets on a stone. The following chart gives examples of written and spoken forms of carat weight:

Written	Spoken
0.005 ct (0.5 pt)	half point
0.05 ct	five points
0.25 ct	twenty-five points or quarter carat
0.50 ct	fifty points or half carat
1.82 ct	one point eight two (carats) or one eighty-two

Note that "point" when used in expressing weights over one carat refers to the decimal point, not a unit of measure. Also note that "pt" can be used instead of "ct" to make people think for example, that a stone weighs 1/2 carat instead 1/2 of a point.

Effect of Carat Weight on Price

Most people are familiar with the principle, the higher the carat weight the greater the value. However, in actual practice, this principle is more complicated than it appears. This can be illustrated by having you determine which emerald ring described below is more valuable. Assume that the quality and shape of all the emeralds are the same and that the two ring mountings have equivalent values.

    a. 1-carat emerald solitaire ring
    b. cocktail ring, 12 emeralds, 1.5 carats TW

Strangely enough, a single 1-carat emerald would normally cost more than 1 1/2 carats of small emeralds of like quality unless the emeralds were low-grade. This is because the supply of large emeralds is more limited. So when you compare jewelry prices, you should pay attention to individual stone weights and **notice the difference between** the labels **1 ct TW** (one carat total weight) **and 1 ct** (the weight of one stone).

When comparing the cost of emeralds and tanzanite, you should also start noting the **per carat cost** instead of concentrating on the total cost of the stone. This makes it easier to compare prices more accurately, which is why dealers buy and sell gems using per-carat prices. The following equations will help you calculate the per-carat cost and total cost of rubies and sapphires.

Per-carat cost = $\dfrac{\text{stone cost}}{\text{carat weight}}$

Total cost of a stone = carat weight x per-carat cost

The per-carat prices of emeralds and tanzanites are listed in terms of either their weight or millimeter size (unlike those of diamonds, which are usually only listed according to carat weight). Emeralds and tanzanites over 1/2 to 3/4 of a carat are generally priced according to weight, whereas those under 1/2 carat tend to be listed in terms of millimeter size.

Price/weight categories for colored stones vary from one dealer to another and the categories are often broader than for diamonds. A one-carat price level for an emerald may extend down to 0.85 carats. Sometimes, a larger weight brings a lower per-carat price. A 50-ct tanzanite, for example, may sell for a little less per carat than an equivalent-quality 10 carater because the smaller stone would be more salable. Similarly, one emerald dealer says he charges less per carat for 2-ct emeralds than for 1 caraters. This is because he has a greater demand for 1-ct emeralds. Some other emerald dealers would disagree. All dealers would probably affirm that a fine 4-ct emerald would cost considerably more per carat than a 1 carater of the same quality.

Since price/weight categories vary from one dealer to another, there's no point in listing any. Just be aware that shape and carat weight can affect the per carat value of emeralds and follow these two guidelines:

♦ Compare per carat prices instead of the total cost.

♦ When judging prices, compare stones of the same size, shape, quality, and color.

Size Versus Carat Weight

Sometimes in the jewelry trade, the term "size" is used as a synonym for "carat weight." This is because size and weight are directly related. However, as emeralds and tanzanites increase in weight, their size becomes less predictable. This means a 0.90-ct emerald, for example, may look bigger than a 1.05-ct emerald. Therefore, you need to consider stone measurements as well as carat weight when buying colored stones. You don't need to carry a millimeter gauge with you when you go shopping. Just start noting the different illusions of size that various stone shapes and measurements can create.

You should also note that emeralds and tanzanites normally have different measurements than other gemstones of the same weight. For example, because of its lower density, a one-carat emerald is considerably larger than a one-carat ruby. The size of a one-carat tanzanite would fall between than of an emerald and a ruby. We can compare gem sizes by comparing their **specific gravitiy** (the ratio of a gem's density to the density of water). The specific gravity of emerald is about 2.72 whereas that of tanzanite is 3.35.

Estimating Carat Weight

If you buy jewelry in a reputable jewelry store, you normally don't need to know how to estimate the carat weight of gems because the weight will be marked. However, if you buy jewelry at flea markets, garage sales, or auctions, it is to your advantage to know how to estimate weight.

One way to estimate the weight of faceted emeralds is to measure their length and width (or diameter) with a millimeter gauge (these are sold at jewelry supply stores). Then match the measurements to those of table 3.3, and look at the corresponding weights. This works best with stones that are small, well-cut, and calibrated (cut to specific sizes). This is not a good way, however, of estimating the weight of stones that have deep bulging pavilions, flat profiles, or odd measurements. It's better to measure their depth as well as the length and width, and then calculate the weight using table 3.4. Of course, the only accurate means of determining the weight of a stone is to take it out of its setting and weigh it. This, however, is not always possible nor advisable.

Table 3.1 Weight Conversions	
1 pennyweight (dwt)	= 1.555 g = 0.05 oz t = 0.055 oz av = 7.776 cts
1 troy ounce (oz t)	= 31.103 g = 1.097 oz av = 20 dwt = 155.51 cts
1 ounce avoirdupois (oz av)	= 28.3495 g = 0.911 oz t = 18.229 dwt = 141.75 cts
1 carat (ct)	= 0.2 g = 0.006 oz t = 0.007 oz av = 0.31 dwt
1 gram (g)	= 5 cts = 0.032 oz t = 0.035 oz av = 0.643 dwt

Table 3.2 Millimeter Sizes (Courtesy Grieger's Inc.)

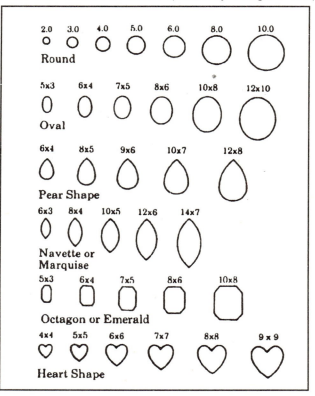

Table 3.3 Shape & Approximate Weights of Calibrated, Faceted Emerald & Tanzanite

Shape	Size mm	Emerald Weight	Tanzanite Weight	Shape	Size mm	Emerald Weight	Tanzanite Weight
Round	2	.03-.04	,04-.05	Emerald Cut	5 x 3	.24-.29	.26-.35
	2.5	.05-.06	..07-.08		6 x 4	.45-.52	.52-.60
	3	.10-.12	.12-.13		6.5 x 4.5	.55-.60	
	3.5	.17-.20	.15-.20		7 x 5	.75-.95	0.95-1.05
	4	.20-.27	.26-.30		7.5 x 5.5	0.95-1.15	
	4.5	.27-.38	.30-.43		8 x 6	1.25-1.50	1.45.1.65
	5	.38-.48	.50-.59		9 x 7	1.85-2.35	2.15-2.45
	5.5	.48-.65	.60-.78		10 x 8	2.80-3.20	3.70-4.00
	6	.65-.80	.85-1.00				
	6.5	.90-.99	1.01-1.27	Oval	5 x 3	.20-.27	.24-.28
	7	1.00-1.24	1.25-1.60		6 x 4	.35-.50	.50-.52
	7.5	1.24-1.60	1.55-1.95		6.5 x 4.5	.45-.55	
					7 x 5	.60-.85	.94-.95
Marquise	6 x 3	.18-.30	.22-.35		8 x 6	0.95-1.24	1.35-1.52
	8 x 4	.43-.52	.50-.53		9 x 7	1.60-1.89	2.00-2.31
	10 x 5	0.85-1.10	1.00-1.04		10 x 8	1.80-2.30	2.50-3.35
	12 x 6	1.40-1.60	2.00		12 x 10	3.60-4.30	
Square	2	.07		Pear	5 x 3	.17-.27	.21-.25
	2.5	.11			6 x 4	.30-.45	.43-.45
	3	.13-.20	.16-.17		7 x 5	.60-.75	.70-.85
	4	.31-.40			8 x 5	0.80-1.05	0.95-1.20
	5	.55-.60	.74		9 x 6	1.10-1.70	
	6	.0.97-1.08	1.29		10 x 7	1.70-2.60	

Note: These weights are only guides. The actual weights can vary. The information in this table is based mostly on size/weight/shape lists of Chatham Created Gems, GRK Gems Inc., Italgem Co., Kashizadeh Co., and *The Professional's Guide to Jewelry Insurance Appraising* by Geolat, Northrup, and Federman, p. 102.

Table 3.4 Weight Estimation Formulas for Faceted Emeralds and Tanzanite	
Rounds	Diameter^2 x depth x S.G. x .0018
Ovals	Diameter^2 x depth x S.G. x .0020 (Average out length and width to get diameter)
Square Cushion	Diameter^2 x depth x S.G. x .0018 (Average out horizontal, vertical, and diagonal measurements for diameter)
Rectangular Cushion	Diameter^2 x depth x S.G. x .0022 (Average length and width to get diameter)
Square Emerald Cut	Average width^2 x depth x S.G. x .0023
Rectangular Emerald Cut	Length x width x depth x S.G. x .0025
Square (with corners)	Average width^2 x depth x S.G. x .0024
Rectangular Baguette	Length x width x depth x S.G. x .0026
Pear	Length x width x depth x S.G. x .0018
Marquise	Length x width x depth x S.G. x .0017
Heart	Length x width x depth x S.G. x .0021

Note: S.G. = Specific Gravity. The specific gravity of emerald is about 2.72 whereas that of tanzanite is about 3.35. The above formulas are based on stones with medium girdles, no pavilion bulge, and well-proportioned shapes. Thick girdles may require a correction of up to 10%. Bulging pavilions may require a correction as high as 18%. The correction for a poor shape outline can be up to 10%.

The above information is based on handouts from the GIA appraisal seminar.

Quiz (Chapters 2 & 3)

1. Which would cost more?

   a. a good tanzanite
   b. a good amethyst
   c. a good blue topaz
   d. a good white (colorless) sapphire

2. Zoisite is:

   a. the place where tanzanite was discovered
   b. a parasite found in East Africa
   c the mineral species of which tanzanite is a member
   d. both a and c

True or False?

3. Colombia, Zambia, and Brazil are major sources of emerald.

4. A 2.5 carat good-quality emerald is worth more than 10 emeralds of the same color and quality which have a total weight of 3 carats.

5. One carat equals 1/5 of a gram.

6. A ten pointer is a stone with ten facet junctions.

7. Emerald is a variety of the mineral species beryl.

8. The first emerald mines recorded in history were in Colombia.

9. A round 1-ct emerald would normally look larger than a round 1-ct tanzanite.

10. When comparing gem prices, you should compare their per-carat cost.

Answer the following questions:

11. If a tanzanite weighs 4 carats and costs $1600, what is its per carat price?

12. What's the total cost of a 1/3 carat emerald which sells for $300 a carat?

See next page for answers

Answers

1. a A good tanzanite would cost a lot more than any of the other three gems.

2. c

3. T

4. T Large good-quality emeralds have a much greater per carat price than small ones of the same quality.

5. T

6. F A ten pointer is a stone that weighs 10 points or 1/10 carat.

7. T

8. F The first recorded emerald mines were in Egypt.

9. T Tanzanite is heavier and has a higher density than emerald. Therefore the emerald would be larger.

10. T

11. $400 $1600 ÷ 4 = $400

12. $100 1/3 X $300 = $100

4

Shape & Cutting Style

The shape and cutting style of an emerald are sometimes linked to its country of origin. Colombian emerald rough typically has the form of a hexagonal cylinder (fig. 4.1). Maximum weight retention is usually achieved by fashioning the rough crystals into emerald cuts, which have a square or rectangular shape, clipped corners, and four-sided facets. Zambian emerald rough, on the other hand, tends to have a rounded shape and is often cut into oval- or pear-shape stones. Sandawana, Zimbabwe emeralds are small and usually round or square.

Tanzanite and emerald are two opposites when it comes to rough sizes and compatibility to particular shapes. Tanzanite rough comes in up to 1 kilogram sizes and many are blocks that lend themselves to nice, accurate saw cuts that give high yields. As a result, tanzanite is found in a wide variety of shapes. One common type is the **cushion shape** which has a squarish or roundish outline with curved sides and rounded corners (fig. 4.2). Ovals, pears, and trilliants (triangles with curved sides) are also typical tanzanite shapes.

Tanzanite and emerald are also occasionally shaped into hearts, kites, shields, hexagons and marquise shapes. Gem cutters try to select shapes and cutting styles which allow them to emphasize preferred colors, minimize undesirable flaws, and/or get the maximum weight yield from the rough. In small calibrated sizes, there is a tendency to cut what the customer wants, even when some shapes cause a greater weight loss.

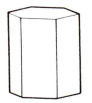

Fig. 4.1 Hexagonal cylinder form. *Diagram courtesy Gemological Institute of America*

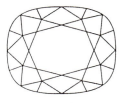

Fig. 4.2 Cushion shape. *Diagram courtesy American Gemological Laboratories*

Fig. 4.3 Top right: Earring set with tapered baguettes and a pear-shape emerald and diamond. *Photo courtesy Harry Winston Inc.*

Fig. 4.4 Left: Platinum ring with an 11.22-ct cushion-cut tanzanite accented by diamond baguettes. The platinum earrings feature removable oval tanzanites. *Photo courtesy Cynthia Renée Co.; photo by Weldon.*

Gemstone Terms Defined

Before you can thoroughly understand a discussion of shapes and cutting styles, some terminology must be explained. A few basic terms are described below and illustrated in figure 4.5.

Facets	The flat, polished surfaces or planes on a stone.
Table	The large, flat top facet. It normally has an octagonal shape on a round stone.
Girdle	The narrow rim around the stone. The girdle plane is parallel to the table and is the largest diameter of any part of the stone.
Crown	The upper part of the stone above the girdle.
Pavilion	The lower part of the stone below the girdle.
Culet	The tiny facet on the pointed bottom of the pavilion, parallel to the table. Sometimes the point of a stone is called "the culet" even if no culet facet is present.
Fancy Shape	Any shape except round. This term is most frequently applied to diamonds.

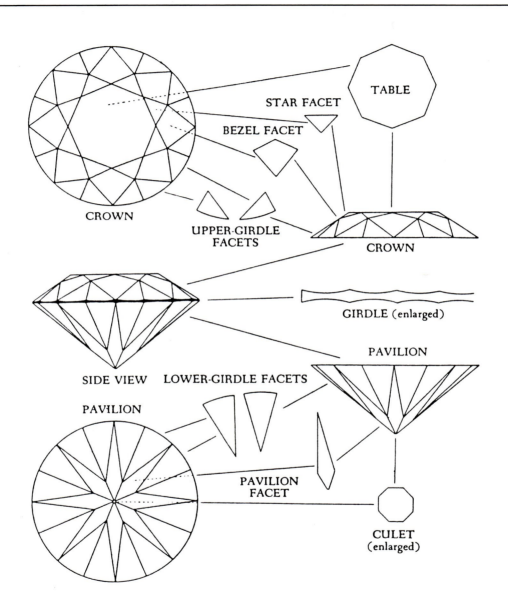

Fig. 4.5 Facet arrangement of a standard round brilliant cut. *Diagram courtesy of the GIA (Gemological Institute of America).*

Cutting Styles

Before the 1300's, gems were usually cut into unfaceted rounded beads or into cabochons (unfaceted dome-shaped stones). Colored gems looked attractive cut this way, but diamonds looked dull. It's thanks to man's interest in bringing out the beauty of diamonds that the art of faceting gemstones was developed. At first, facets were added haphazardly, but by around 1450, diamonds began to be cut with a symmetrical arrangement of facets. Various styles gradually evolved, and by the 1920's, the modern round-brilliant cut was popular.

As cutters discovered how faceting could bring out the brilliance and sparkle of diamonds, they started to apply the same techniques to colored stones. Today, emeralds and tanzanite are cut into the following styles:

Step Cut   Has rows of facets which are cut parallel to the edges and resemble the steps of a staircase. Emerald is commonly fashioned into small step-cut **squares** or **baguettes** (square-cornered, rectangular stones) (fig. 4.4 & 4.6). If step-cuts have corners which have been clipped off, they're called **emerald cuts** because emeralds are often cut this way (figs. 4.7-4.9). This protects the corners and provides places where prongs can secure the stone. Even though step-cut tanzanite is available (fig. 4.9), it is more frequently fashioned into the mixed-cut or brilliant-cut styles.

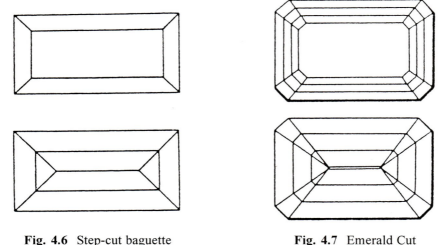

Fig. 4.6 Step-cut baguette   **Fig. 4.7** Emerald Cut

Fig. 4.8 This elegant necklace is composed of marquise-shaped diamonds and emeralds with an emerald-cut style. The emerald in the pendant is a step-cut square weighing 37 carats. *The necklace is courtesy Harry Winston Inc.; photo © Harold & Erica Van Pelt.*

Fig. 4.9 A 33-ct emerald-cut tanzanite. It might retail for about $30,000. (Daylight equivalent lighting)

Brilliant Cut Has mostly 3-sided facets which radiate outward from the stone (fig. 4.10). Kite- or lozenge-shaped facets may also be present. The best-known example is the **full-cut round brilliant**, which has 58 facets (fig. 4.5). Ovals, pears, marquises, and heart-shapes can also be brilliant-cut. The **single cut**, which has 17 or 18 facets, is another type of brilliant cut. It may be found on small stones, often of low quality, or on imitations. Square stones cut in the brilliant style are called **princess cuts**. Triangular brilliant cuts are called **trilliants**.

The princess and trilliant cuts were originally developed for diamonds because their brilliant-style facets create a greater amount of brilliance and sparkle than step facets do. Now the princess and trilliant cuts are becoming popular for some colored stones. Emeralds are not normally cut in a full-brilliant style. Cuts such as the step and mixed cut intensify their color more effectively.

Mixed cut Has both step- and brilliant-cut facets (fig. 4.11). This is a popular faceting style for both emerald and tanzanite. The crown is brilliant cut to maximize brilliance and hide flaws if present (fig. 3.16). The pavilion on the other hand is either entirely step cut or else has a combination of both step- and brilliant-type facets. The step facets allow cutters to save weight and bring out the color of the stone. Occasionally, the mixed cut is referred to as the **Ceylon cut**.

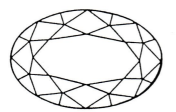
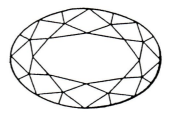
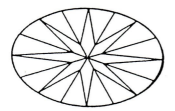
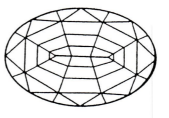

Fig. 4.10 Oval brilliant cut   **Fig. 4.11** Oval mixed cut

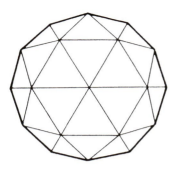

Fig. 4.12 Top left: The **rose cut** has triangular brilliant-style facets, a pointed dome-shaped crown, a flat base, and a circular girdle outline. This cut, which probably originated in India, was introduced into Europe by Venetian polishers in the fifteenth century.

Fig. 4.13 Top right: Three rose-cut emeralds and a 65-ct briolette emerald valued at $210,000. A **briolette** has a tear-drop shape, a circular cross-section, and triangular facets (or occasionally rectangular, step-cut-style facets). *Photo courtesy Harry Winston, Inc.*

Fig. 4.14 An oval mixed-cut tanzanite secured with well-crafted prongs. The four-sided pavilion facets are visible through the table of the stone. Triangular crown facets add sparkle to the stone. *Photo courtesy Tiffany & Co.*

Bead (faceted & unfaceted) — Usually has a ball-shaped form with a hole through the center. Most faceted beads have either brilliant- or step-type facets. Emerald beads are generally made from non-transparent or heavily flawed material.

Cabochon Cut — Has a dome-shaped top and either a flat or rounded bottom. This is the simplest cut for a stone and is often seen in antique jewelry. Today this cut tends to be used for opaque, translucent, and star & cat's-eye stones. Transparent emeralds with lots of flaws are also frequently cut into cabochons. **Trapiche emeralds**, which have a six-rayed star pattern formed by black inclusions, are also cut into cabochons. *Trapiche* is the Spanish word for the cogwheel used to grind sugar cane, which has an appearance similar to these emeralds.

Fig. 4.15 Cabochon emerald bezel-set in a platinum ring. *Photo courtesy Maurice Badler Fine Jewelry; photo by the Goldmark Group.*

Fig. 4.16 A 15.2-ct trapiche emerald ring. *Photo by Howard Rubin.*

Carvings and sculptures — The first emerald carvings originated in ancient Egypt when emeralds were carved into good-luck charms and scarabs (gems that resembled a beetle). Throughout history, emeralds have been engraved with portraits, floral patterns, landscapes, and inscriptions of religious verses and prayers. India, in particular, is noted for its fine emerald carvings.

No large emerald sculptures were created until the 16th century, when huge crystals from Colombia became available. The first sculptures that have been recorded were those brought back to Spain from the New World by Hernando Cortez. Among these treasures were a cup edged in gold, a bell fitted with a fine pearl as the clapper, and a fish with eyes of gold, all carved out of emerald. The Queen of Spain wanted these sculptures, but Cortez refused to part with them and gave her other jewels instead. She wasn't satisfied. As a result, Cortez's influence in the court declined. Later, Cortez lost the emerald carvings when his vessel was wrecked at sea. (From *Emerald & Other Beryls* by John Sinkankas, pages 115-116).

A non-crystal form of nontransparent green zoisite containing ruby is often carved into colorful ornaments. (Green zoisite and tanzanite are varieties of the gem species zoisite.)

How Shape & Cutting Style Affect Price

Color, clarity and brilliance normally play a greater role in determining the price of an emerald or tanzanite than shape and cutting style. Nevertheless, these two factors can affect the value of these stones. The way they affect it is described below.

Since the **cabochon** is the simplest style, it costs less to cut than faceted styles. Another reason cabochons are generally priced less is that they are often made from lower quality material that is unsuitable for faceting. Cabochon stones can also be of high quality, especially those found in antique jewelry.

The shape of **faceted** emeralds can have a greater effect on their price than the faceting style. Good-quality round emeralds with the same measurement as a 1-carat diamond usually sell for a premium. This is because large round emeralds are relatively rare, and they look attractive when set with a round diamond of equal size. Also, more weight is normally lost from the rough when cutting round emeralds. There are cases, however, where round stones may cost less than an emerald cut. A high-quality, 4-carat round emerald may be harder to sell than an emerald cut. In this case, the stone with the greater demand would cost more per carat.

Well-matched emeralds with an unusual shape such as a heart can also sell for a premium if they are of high quality. As a group, the stones are worth more per carat than if sold individually. A good example of this is the emerald necklace in figure 4.17. Sometimes it takes years to collect so many well-matched stones of the same shape.

Emerald dealers don't always agree on which shapes are the most valuable. The marquise shape is the most controversial. Some dealers claim the marquise is the lowest priced emerald shape because there is little demand for it. Others say the marquise shape

Fig. 4.17 A distinctive necklace set with 15 emeralds weighing 68 carats. The emeralds in the earrings have a total weight of 18 carats. It's amazing that so many well-matched, heart shapes of high quality were found for this necklace. Emeralds are not frequently cut into heart shapes. *Photo courtesy Harry Winston Inc.*

costs the most because it's rare and doesn't yield much weight from the rough. However, most would agree that if someone called to request a marquise, its price could go up.

Shape is less of a price factor in tanzanite than in emerald. The trilliant, though, can cost 10 to 15% more than the oval and cushion cuts because it's a popular shape with a low yield from the rough. Rounds may also sell at a premium due to their low weight yield. Pear shapes sometimes cost less because they are readily available and give the best yield on account of tanzanite cleavage. Stones of low quality are generally priced alike regardless of their shape.

Cutting style can also play a role in tanzanite pricing. A lot of tanzanite is precision cut in Idar-Oberstein, Germany with unusual faceting patterns. These stones cost more per carat mainly because of the greater amount of skill and time required to cut them. Stones cut by equally skilled cutters in other countries can command the same prices.

Beads, even when faceted, are generally priced lower than other cuts because they tend to be made of inferior material. Although in the past, some high quality emerald has been used for beads, it wouldn't make sense today to decrease the weight and value of fine quality emerald by drilling holes through it. Consequently, emerald beads are often made from nontransparent or heavily flawed material which isn't suitable for other cuts.

Carved emeralds and tanzanite are usually priced per piece instead of per carat. Their value varies according to the skill and fame of the cutter, the quality of the material used, the time required to execute their design, the fame of their owner(s), and their antique value.

It would be pointless to contrast the prices of carvings to the prices of the other cuts. Each carving should be judged on its own artistic merits. When judging the prices of other cuts, keep in mind that it's best to compare stones of the same cutting style as well as the same shape, size, color, and clarity. This will help you judge value more accurately.

5

Judging Emerald Color

Muzo is the most famous of Colombia's emerald mines. It has produced stones of matchless beauty for more than 1000 years. The rare, fine, saturated green crystals sometimes found there are the yard-stick by which all other emeralds are judged.
    (*Emeralds of the World*, pg 33, by Jules Roger Sauer, Brazilian gem dealer and mine owner.)

The color of the finest Muzo emeralds has been described by some as "grass green." This is not a good description. Grasses come in a wide range of greens which tend to be grayish or brownish. The finest Muzo emeralds are noted for having a much purer green color. Examine a blade of grass from your lawn, and you'll probably agree that it does not have a top-grade emerald color.

For a more precise and accurate description of emeralds, color must be divided into three main components.

Hue	Refers to basic colors like blue, green, and yellow as well as transition colors like bluish green and yellowish green.
Lightness/darkness (Tone)	Refers to the depth of color. The lightest possible tone is colorless. The darkest is black. **Tone** is another word for the degree of lightness or darkness. It will be described in this book by the following terms:

        very light
        light
        medium light
        medium
        medium dark
        dark
        very dark

Color purity　　　The degree to which the hue is masked by brown or gray. This book will describe color purity loosely with terms such as "highly pure" and "slightly brownish or grayish."

Color purity is termed **saturation** in the GIA color grading system, and colors with a minimum amount of brown or gray are described as **vivid** or **strong.** The American Gemological Laboratories (AGL) uses **intensity** to refer to color purity.

The terms **saturation** and **intensity** have other meanings. When dealers such as Jules Sauer describe the color of fine emeralds as a saturated green, they often mean that the stones have both a high purity and good depth of color (tone). To these dealers, a light pure green emerald is neither saturated, nor strong, nor intense green.

"Saturation" sometimes only refers to the tone of pure colors. This is how it is used in GemDialogue, a color reference system used by many appraisers and jewelers,

In this book, "saturated" and "intense" refer to both the tone and purity of color. Emerald colors described with these terms will have a medium to medium-dark tone with a minimal amount of gray or brown masking the hue.

Before proceeding with an evaluation of emerald color, this book must also define what it means by "emerald." "Emerald" is another term whose meaning varies depending on the user.

Emerald or Green Beryl?

Prior to the mid-18th century, very little was known about the physical and chemical properties of emerald. As a result, the term "emerald" was applied to almost any green gemstone, be it emerald, green tourmaline, or green sapphire.

In 1798, the French chemist Nicolas Louis Vauquelin published the first reasonably accurate chemical analysis of emerald. Thanks to Vauquelin's research, emerald could be classified as a member of the gem species **beryl** ($Be_3Al_2Si_6O_{18}$) along with the following varieties:

aquamarine　　　very light to medium light blue to bluish green beryl. There's no agreed upon dividing line between aquamarine and light-colored emerald.

morganite　　　pink or orange beryl

goshenite   colorless beryl

golden beryl   also called heliodor or yellow beryl

red beryl   sometimes called bixbite or incorrectly, red emerald. By defini-
                       tion an emerald is a green stone.

maxixe beryl   medium to dark blue which fades in light

The fact that emerald is beryl which is green could lead one to believe that "green beryl" and "emerald" are synonymous. These terms can, however, have different meanings that change with the user. Four factors can play a role in the distinction between green beryl and emerald. They are:

Hue   According to the GIA Colored Stone Grading System, the hue range of emeralds is bluish green through green. The GIA classifies slightly yellowish-green emeralds and yellowish-green emeralds as green beryl. (*GIA Gem Reference Guide*, pg 33, and GIA Colored Stone Grading Course Charts, 1992 version.)
                       Gem dealers, on the other hand, consider yellowish-green beryl to be emerald.

Tone   Some dealers call light green emerald "green beryl" and reserve the term "emerald" for darker tones. Many other dealers label any green beryl as emerald.
                       The GIA Colored Stone Grading course has established the tonal range of emeralds as light to very dark. Very light stones are termed "green beryl."

Color Purity   Most grayish and slightly grayish emeralds are classified by the GIA as green beryl. Slightly grayish emeralds that are medium dark to very dark may be called emerald. (GIA Colored Stone Grading Course Charts, 1992 version).
                       Dealers generally regard both grayish- or brownish-green emerald as emerald of inferior quality.

Coloring Agent   The body color of most transparent colored gems is due to me-tallic elements (**coloring agents**) present in their crystal structure. Beryl can take on a green color if its chemical make-up consists of chromium, vanadium, and/or iron impurities.
                       Many prominent European gemologists have maintained that emerald must be colored by chromium to merit the name

"emerald." Otherwise it is green beryl. For example, in *Emeralds of Pakistan* (pg 75), Dr. Eduard Gübelin writes: "The green beryls from Gandao cannot be regarded as emerald because their green color is not imparted by Cr_2O_3 (chromium) but exclusively by V_2O_3 (vanadium)."

Australian gemologist I. A. Mumme even feels that the percentage of chromium present is important. He states in his book *The Emerald* (pg 86) "Emerald is beryl ($Be_3Al_2Si_6O_{18}$) which contains 0.3-1% chromium impurity."

According to the GIA, emerald can be colored by chromium, vanadium, or both elements. Stones colored by iron would be classified as green beryl. (*GIA Gem Reference Guide*, pp 28 & 33).

If a dealer differentiates green beryl from emerald, his classification will normally be based on the color of the stone, not its coloring agents.

In this book the term **emerald** refers to all beryl ranging from bluish green to yellowish green regardless of its tone, color purity, or coloring agent. The author's reasons for not distinguishing between green beryl and emerald are as follows:

◆ It's easier to explain emerald evaluation to consumers when all beryl that is green is called emerald. For example, the phrase "light green emeralds cost less than those which are medium green" is more meaningful to the layperson than "light green beryl costs less than medium green emerald."

◆ At gem shows and in stores, any beryl that looks more or less green is typically labeled "emerald."

◆ Many respected gemologists (particularly those in Europe) do not classify an emerald as green beryl just because it's yellowish, grayish, or pale. Dr. Eduard Gübelin indicates this when he describes a parcel of Pakistani emeralds. "The specimens ranged between a low quality of pale green to grayish green hue marred by numerous inclusions rendering them translucent rather than transparent, and a very fine quality of an exquisite bluish or yellowish green shade, highly transparent with only very few inclusions." (*Emeralds of Pakistan* (pg 75).

◆ There's no practical way for jewelers and dealers to determine the coloring agent(s) of all their emeralds.

◆ There are no agreed-upon criteria in the trade for distinguishing between green beryl and emerald.

Evaluating Emerald Color

Even though it's debatable as to what are the most valuable emerald hues and tones, gem dealers agree that pure colors are more desirable than dull, muddy ones. In high-quality emeralds, the bright areas of color should not look grayish or brownish.

Fig. 5.1 Two high-quality emeralds with good color saturation. Their actual color may be a bit different because the printing & developing processes usually alter the true color of gems in photos. *Photo courtesy Harry Winston Inc.*

Judging the **lightness or darkness** of faceted gemstones is difficult because they don't display a single, uniform tone. To judge the tone of a faceted emerald, examine it face-up and answer the following questions:

♦ What is your first overall impression of the tone? How does it compare to that of other emeralds you have seen? Use words such as "light" and "medium light" to describe tone, but keep in mind that the tonal boundaries of these terms can vary from one person and grading system to another.

The depth of color plays a major role in the price of an emerald. For example, a pure deep-green emerald selling for $5000 might be worth less than $100 if it were very light green. There's nothing inherently wrong, though, with light-green emeralds. In fact, they can be quite flattering to people who look good in pastel colors. It's just that there is a much greater demand for deep green emeralds and their supply is more limited.

◆ Do you see near colorless, washed-out areas in the stone? This is a symbol of insufficient color, poor cutting or both.

◆ What percentage of the emerald looks black? If more than 90% of the stone is blackish, gem dealers would classify it as undesirable. Your first impression of an emerald should be that it's green, not black.

The GIA refers to the dark black or gray areas seen through the crown of faceted gems as **extinction**.. The amount of extinction you see depends on the tone, the cut, the type of lighting and the distance of the light from the stone. Light-colored, shallow-cut stones normally show less extinction than those which are dark and/or deep-cut. As the light source gets broader, more diffused, and/or closer to stones, they display less extinction and more color.

When grading color, you should view stones about 12 inches (30.4cm) below a neutral fluorescent light such as the Duro-Test Vita light, GE Chroma 50 or Sylvania Design 50. Under these conditions, an emerald with a medium-dark tone would typically have about 35 to 50% extinction, according to the GIA definition of medium dark. A lot of high-quality emeralds fall in this range.

There is a difference of opinion as to what is the ideal tone for an emerald. According to the GIA, the most valued emeralds have a medium tone. Some dealers, however, prefer medium-dark emeralds because their bright areas may appear more saturated in color. One can conclude that top-grade emeralds range in tone from medium to medium-dark.

Judging the **hue** of an emerald is just as hard as judging the tone since emeralds can display different hues and tones simultaneously. Moreover, emeralds are a blend of two colors--bluish green and yellowish green. If you look at an emerald from different directions while moving it, you may be able to see these two colors.

Examine the stone face up when judging hue. Look for the average or dominant color reflected in the bright facet areas inside the stone. The GIA Colored Stone Grading Course rates bluish green as the most valued emerald hue. As with tone, trade members differ on which hue(s) they consider best.

New York emerald dealer Robert Shire, for example, prefers slightly yellowish-green emeralds. He feels that a yellowish tint gives an emerald a warm feeling. To him a bluish-green color tends to be cold. He believes, too, that hue is a matter of preference.

For Jack Abraham, a New York gem dealer, "green-green" is the ideal hue. He also feels that hue is a matter of taste and goes on to say that many of the finest Muzo emeralds are slightly bluish.

John Sinkankas and Peter Read, both noted for their research in gemology and mineralogy, suggest that bluish green is the best emerald hue. In their book *Beryl*, they explain that emeralds are cut so that "the colour seen in such a gem is largely the blueish-green prized by most connoisseurs of emeralds above the yellowish-green that would appear if the gem were cut with the table perpendicular to the c-axis" pg 102).

Yasukazu Suwa, Japanese gemologist and gem dealer, implies that strongly bluish stones are less desirable when he writes "(Zambian emeralds) are cut to sizes exceeding 2 carats, but these lack the warmth of Colombian material, perhaps due to their homogenous color, exhibiting a cooler hue which is strongly blue." (*Gemstones: Quality and Value*, pg 40.

In the same book, Yasukazu Suwa writes: "Colombian emeralds possess a soft, beautiful green. They may be slightly bluish or yellowish, but they are close to pure in color with no evidence of grayishness that lowers the intensity of their color" (pg 34). He describes the color of the Sandawana emeralds of Zimbabwe as a "beautiful yellowish green" pg 44.

I. A. Mumme writes in his book *The Emerald*, "For those who prefer the spectro-scope as a method of testing the colour of an emerald, a colour about 5000A (i.e. slightly towards the bluish-end of the green portion of the white light spectrum) would be very close an approximation to the colour of fine emerald. Another prize colour being accepted by gem valuators today is the deep yellow green colour of Sandawana emeralds" pg 130.

In his book *Gems*, the noted British gemologist Robert Webster wrote, "The yellowish-green stones from the Muzo district have a warm velvety appearance which is most prized" (pg 104, 4th edition).

In the early stages of this book, the author believed that the finest emeralds were a slightly bluish green. Later, after further research, she concluded that there is a range of "top emerald colors" centering around green. Howard Rubin, a former gem dealer, also feels that premium colors can range from slightly bluish green to slightly yellowish green. He stated this in 1986 in a manual accompanying the GemDialogue color matching charts he developed.

When emerald color is discussed, the country of origin is invariably mentioned. Some dealers say they can often tell where a stone is from just by its color. There's good reason for this. The coloring agent(s) of emeralds can vary from one locality to another. The green of Columbian emeralds, for example, is caused by chromium whereas Brazilian emeralds of good quality are generally colored by vanadium. The coloring agent of light-colored Brazilian emeralds is frequently iron.

Fig. 5.2

Fig. 5.3

Fig. 5.4

Figs. 5.2 to 5.4 Three different color separations of a 4-ct Muzo emerald, which wholesales for about $30,000. A layperson may not notice the various nuances of color but an emerald dealer will. The emerald in figure 5.3 is a bit lighter than the first one in figure 5.2. The lower emerald in figure 5.4 is slightly more yellowish than the other two. Danny and Ronny Levy, the owners of this stone, preferred the color proof of figure 5.2. After this book is printed, their opinion could change. At each stage of the printing and developing processes, slight color changes usually occur.

Even though characteristic emerald colors are associated with different regions, you should keep in mind that there can be a wide variation of color within each emerald mine. Don't assume that just because an emerald is from Columbia, it is of high quality. Neither should you assume that it is inferior if found outside of Colombia. Many fine-quality emeralds have originated in Africa, Brazil, or Pakistan. You must judge each stone on its own merits.

How to Examine Color

When selecting an emerald, follow these steps:

♦ First, clean the stone with a soft cloth if it's dirty. Dirt and fingerprints hide color and brilliance.

♦ Examine the stone face up against a variety of backgrounds. Look straight down at it over a non-reflective, white background and check if the center of the stone is pale and washed out. (This is undesirable). Then look at it against a black background. Do you still see glints of green or does most of the color disappear? Also, check how good the stone looks next to your skin.

♦ Examine the stone under direct light and away from it. Your emerald won't always be spotlighted as you wear it. Does it still look green out of direct light? It should if it's of good quality.

♦ Look at the stone under various types of light available in the store. For example, check the color under an incandescent light-bulb, fluorescent light, and next to a window. If you're trying to match stones, it's particularly important to view them together under different lights. Stones that match under one light source may be mismatched under another.

  Incandescent lighting enhances the color of emeralds, making them look greener. That's why they are said to be an ideal night stone.

♦ Every now and then, look away from the emeralds and glance at other colors and objects to give your eyes a rest. When you focus too long on one color, your perception of it is distorted.

♦ Examine the stone from the side to check for **color zoning**--the uneven distribution of color. When the color is uneven or concentrated in one spot, this can sometimes decrease the stone's value. It can also present a problem if the stone is recut. The color may become lighter. Obvious color zoning is most serious when visible in the face-up view of a stone.

♦ Compare the stone side-by-side with other emeralds. Color nuances will be more apparent.

♦ Make sure you're alert and feel good when you examine stones. If you're tired, sick, or under the influence of alcohol or drugs, your perception of color will be impaired.

Grading Color in Emeralds Versus Diamonds

Grading color in emeralds would be much easier if a scale of 23 letter grades could adequately describe their color differences. Diamond color is graded with a scale like this extending from D to Z. The jewelry trade, however, has not yet adopted a standardized system for grading colored stones. The following comparisons of diamond/emerald color grades and characteristics will help you understand why.

♦ Diamond color grades only need to indicate the amount of color present (the tone). Emerald color grades must also describe the hue and color purity to adequately explain price differences.

♦ Diamond color grades represent a smaller range of tones than is needed for emeralds. The highest priced diamond tone, D, is colorless. Their lowest priced tone, Z, is light yellow. The tonal range of emeralds extends from very light to very dark.

♦ Diamond color grades are based mainly on the side view of the stone. Emerald color grades are based mainly on the face-up view, which due to its many reflections is much harder to judge.

♦ Diamonds nearly always have one hue, if they are not colorless. Emeralds can exhibit two hues simultaneously, bluish green and yellowish green, which complicates color grading. The cutting makes a difference in how these two hues combine in the face-up position. In certain directions, only one of the two colors is visible. The technical term for this two-color effect in emerald is **dichroism.**

♦ Diamonds can be color-graded against master diamonds. Emerald color comparison is most often done using plastic, synthetic, and/or foil materials. These substances display color and reflect light differently than emerald, so the color grading of emeralds is harder.

   Some dealers use emeralds from their own inventory for color comparison. They feel accurate emerald grading is best achieved by referring to other emeralds. Assembling uniform sets of master emeralds, however, would be extremely expensive and time-consuming considering all their variations of hue, tone, and color purity. As a result, no one has developed emerald master sets for general use.

♦ The lack of color is what's important in diamonds (unless they're fancy-colored diamonds). The quality of the color is what's important in emeralds; and for simplicity's sake, the descriptive terms used should be applicable to all other colored gemstones for color comparison purposes. Naturally, a grading system that includes all colored stones will be far more complex than one just designed for diamonds.

6

Judging Clarity & Transparency

The disparity between the value of a perfect and of an imperfect emerald is enormous. A faultless emerald is worth as much, or nearly as much, as a ruby, and certainly more than a diamond...As a matter of fact, a perfect emerald weighing but a few carats is so rare that almost any price will be given for it by collectors.
(1896, Dr. Max Bauer, German mineralogist, from his book *Precious Stones*, p. 309.)

Red diamonds have now surpassed rubies and emeralds in value, but Dr. Bauer's comments about emerald clarity are still valid today. Clarity and transparency are very important value factors, sometimes even more important than color. No matter how grayish, brownish, and/or light-colored an emerald is, it's still a gem if it's transparent and **eye-clean** (free of flaws visible to the unaided eye). However, if an emerald is opaque and filled with long deep cracks and eye-visible flaws, it is an industrial grade stone, even if it has a desirable color.

Emeralds typically have some eye-visible flaws. Tanzanite, on the other hand, is normally eye clean. As a result, there is a greater tolerance for noticeable flaws in emerald than in tanzanite. This chapter will not only show you how emeralds and tanzanite differ in clarity; it will also help you make judgments about gemstone flaws. But first, some basic terminology should be explained.

Clarity is the degree to which a stone is free from flaws. Gemologists call flaws within a stone **inclusions**. Flaws on a stone's surface are **blemishes**. A general term for inclusions and blemishes is **clarity characteristics.** In this book, *flaw* is the term normally used because it is shorter and clearer. Some trade members believe the use of the word *flaw* creates customer resistance to gems. When inclusions and blemishes are properly explained, it doesn't matter what they are called. Customers will learn to accept them as a normal characteristic of natural gemstones. Flaws do generally have a negative impact on value, but this is good news for the buyer. They can make a gem more affordable, without necessarily affecting its beauty.

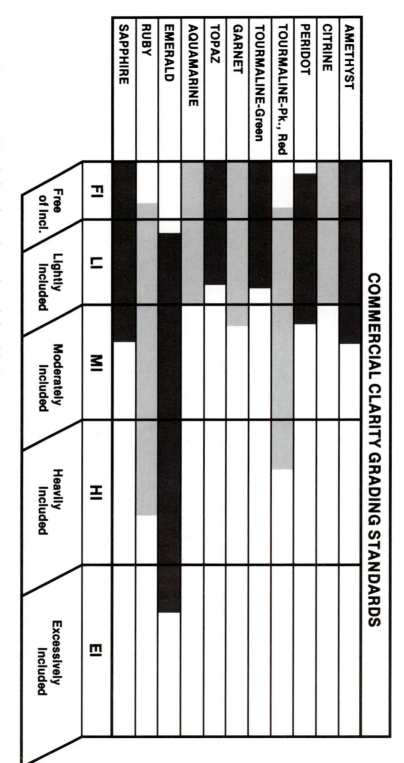

COMMERCIAL CLARITY GRADING STANDARDS

	Free of Incl.	Lightly Included	Moderately Included	Heavily Included	Excessively Included
	FI	LI	MI	HI	EI
AMETHYST					
CITRINE					
PERIDOT					
TOURMALINE-Pk., Red					
TOURMALINE-Green					
GARNET					
TOPAZ					
AQUAMARINE					
EMERALD					
RUBY					
SAPPHIRE					

Table 6.1 This clarity chart shows the relationship between various colored stones and indicates the limits of clarity that are generally acceptable to most jewelry manufacturers and stone dealers. A heavily flawed ruby, for example, is more salable than a sapphire of the same clarity. Emeralds generally have more flaws than other gemstones. *Diagram copyright 1976 by AGL (American Gemological Laboratories).*

Transparency is the degree to which light passes through a material so that objects are visible through it. Transparency and clarity are interlinked because flaws can block the passage of light. Gemologists use the following terms to describe gem transparency.

♦ **Transparent**--objects seen through the stone look clear and distinct.

♦ **Semitransparent**--objects look slightly hazy or blurry through the stone.

♦ **Translucent**--objects are vague and hard to see. Imagining what it is like to read print through frosted glass will help you understand the concept of translucency.

♦ **Semitranslucent**--only a small fraction of light passes through the stone, mainly around the edges.

♦ **Opaque**--virtually no light passes through the stone.

Another word that refers to transparency is **texture.** AGL (American Gemological Laboratories) in New York applies this term to fine particles which interrupt the passage of light in a material. The finely divided particles are not detrimental to the durability of a stone, but they can have an adverse effect on its appearance. Texture is not always a negative factor. The texture within Kashmir sapphire gives it a prized velvety appearance. AGL, on its lab documents, describes the texture (transparency) of colored stones as follows:.

♦ Faint texture: very slightly hazy
♦ Moderate texture: cloudy
♦ Strong texture: translucent
♦ Prominent texture: semi-translucent or opaque

Dealers often use other terms to designate the transparency of an emerald, some of which are:

♦ crystal (highly transparent)   ♦ looks like jade
♦ highly transparent   ♦ looks like soap
♦ milky   ♦ has poor (or low) transparency
♦ cloudy

If this were a book solely on tanzanite, there would be no need to discuss transparency, because tanzanite, unlike most emerald, is very transparent. However, when emeralds are described, both the clarity and transparency are often indicated. For example, top quality Pakistani emeralds are characterized as being "highly transparent with only very few inclusions" by Eduard Gübelin (*Emeralds of Pakistan*, pg 75). In *Gemstones: Quality and Value*, Yasukazu Suwa states "The main factors that might lower the beauty grade of Colombian emeralds are low transparency and an abundance of imperfections" (pg 34).

Inclusions in Natural Emerald and Tanzanite

♦ **Cracks** of various sizes are a normal occurrence in emeralds. In tanzanite, they're only seen occasionally. When cracks are jagged, they're termed **fractures**. A crack is called a **cleavage** if it's straight, flat and parallel to a crystal plane. Tanzanite has one direction of perfect cleavage, which means if you hit it hard in that direction, the stone may easily break.

Emeralds can also break, but this is normally due to existing fractures, not cleavage. Metallic impurities are believed to be a possible cause of the cracks often found in emerald. In the *Photoatlas of Gemstone Inclusions*, Eduard Gübelin and John Koivula state "The admixture of some chromium, which grants the emerald its superb green hue, and a slightly increased amount of Mg and Na, could be responsible for the above-average brittleness, which fosters the multitude of inclusions" (pg 244).

Because of their appearance, cracks are sometimes referred to as **feathers**.

♦ **Crystals** are solid mineral inclusions of various shapes and sizes (figs 6.1 & 6.5). Minute crystals are sometimes called **pinpoints** or **grains**.

♦ **Negative crystals or voids** are hollow spaces inside a stone that have the shape of a crystal. They often resemble solid crystals, so for purposes of clarity grading, they're just called "included crystals."

♦ **Needles** are long, thin inclusions that are either solid crystals or tubes filled with gas or liquid, which are called **growth tubes**. Needles are found in both emerald and tanzanite (fig. 6.2).

♦ **Liquid inclusions** are hollow spaces filled with fluid. Together with fractures, they are the most common emerald inclusions. They occur in random shapes and sometimes are so dense that the stone may look milky. In emeralds, they often resemble mossy growths or "gardens."

Liquid inclusions are classified into three types: **single-phase**, a void containing only liquid; **two-phase**, a liquid and a gas or two nonmixable liquids; and **three-phase**, a liquid, a gas, and a solid (figs. 6.3 & 6.4). These inclusions can provide clues about the origin of an emerald. Colombian emeralds, for example, are noted for their jagged-edged three-phase inclusions which contain a salty liquid, gas bubble(s), and salt (halite) crystal(s). Indian emeralds often have parallel two-phase inclusions.

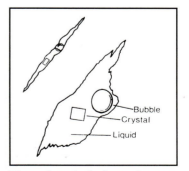

Three-phase inclusions. Courtesy Gemological Institute of America.

Fig. 6.1 Crystal inclusions in emerald

Fig. 6.2 Needle inclusions in tanzanite

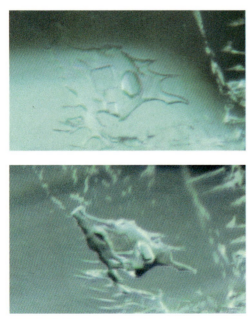

Figs. 6.3 & 6.4 A three-phase inclusion in a Colombian emerald viewed with two types of lighting. In the upper photo, it is only lit from the bottom. In the lower one, overhead lighting was also used.

Fig. 6.5 A crystal and fingerprint inclusion in tanzanite

◆ **Fingerprints** are partially healed cracks (fig. 6.5). Emeralds and tanzanite grow from a mineral solution, and if they split during formation, the solution can fill the cracks and let them grow back together. During this healing process, stray drops of liquid are sealed in and form patterns that look like human fingerprints.

◆ **Growth or color zoning** refers to an uneven distribution of color in a stone. If the different color zones look like bands, they are called **growth or color bands**. Colombian emeralds are frequently color zoned.

◆ **Cavities** are holes or indentations extending into a stone from the surface. Cavities can result when solid crystals are pulled out of a stone or when negative crystals are exposed during the cutting process.

◆ **Chips** are notches or broken off pieces of stone along the girdle edge or at the culet.

Surface Blemishes on Emeralds and Tanzanite

◆ **Scratches** are straight or crooked lines scraped on a stone. Since they can be polished away, they don't have much of an effect on the clarity grade.

◆ **Pits** are tiny holes on the surface of a stone that often look like white dots.

◆ **Abrasions** are rough, scraped areas usually along the facet edges of a stone. They are seen more often on colored stones than on a diamond, due to the diamond's exceptional hardness.

How Lighting Can Affect Your Perception of Clarity

You should judge the clarity of colored stones using overhead lighting both with and without magnification. A loupe (hand magnifier) or a microscope can help you see potentially damaging flaws that might escape the unaided eye.

When people use microscopes to judge clarity, they usually examine the stones with a lighting called **darkfield illumination**. This is a diffused lighting which comes up diagonally through the bottom of the stone. (A frosted or shaded bulb provides **diffused** light, a clear bulb does not.) In this lighting, tiny inclusions and even dust particles will stand out in high relief. As a result, the clarity of the stone appears worse than it would under normal conditions (figures 6.6 to 6.12 provide examples of this).

Overhead lighting is above the stone (not literally over a person's head). It is reflected off the facets whereas darkfield lighting is transmitted through the stone. When looking at jewelry with the unaided eye, you normally view it in overhead lighting. However, if you ask salespeople to show you a stone under a microscope, it is unlikely

How Lighting and Positioning Affect Your Perception of Clarity

Fig. 6.6 1-carat Colombian emerald under overhead lighting. Though not fine quality, this emerald has relatively good transparency and clarity. Its retail value is about $3000 per carat.

Fig. 6.7 Same emerald tilted differently. The "window" through the stone is smaller, but the emerald looks more flawed and less transparent than in figure 6.6.

Fig 6.8 Approximate size

Fig. 6.9 Same emerald in darkfield illumination. A layperson might think this is a reject when in fact, it's a good emerald. The white rectangular areas along the edge are light reflections.

Fig. 6.10 The emerald does not look any better when the background is changed to a light color. The light coming up diagonally through the stone still exaggerates the flaws.

Note: The actual color and clarity of this stone are probably different than shown. The printing and developing processes usually alter detail, contrast, and the true color of gems in photographs.

Fig. 6.11 A tanzanite in overhead light. From the standpoint of appearance, the clarity is not bad. However, the central crack is a durability threat, especially since tanzanite cleaves so easily.

Fig. 6.12 Darkfield illumination turns a hardly noticeable "fingerprint" into a distracting inclusion. Ten-power magnification through a microscope was used for this stone in both photos.

that they will use its overhead lamp. Instead they may only have you view the stone under darkfield illumination.

When judging colored-stone clarity under magnification, you should use overhead lighting for the following reasons:

♦ **Dealers use overhead lighting when pricing gems**. They typically examine stones under a fluorescent lamp with and without a loupe (usually 10-power).

♦ **Overhead illumination is a natural way of lighting which does not exaggerate flaws.** It therefore helps you make a fair assessment of a stone's appearance.

♦ **Overhead lighting does not hide brilliance**. The prime reason for looking at gems through loupes and microscopes is to see their beauty and brilliance magnified. Darkfield illumination masks brilliance. Consequently, it prevents you from making an accurate global assessment of a gem under magnification.

After using overhead lighting, you should also view stones (particularly emeralds) under darkfield illumination. It highlights inclusion details which are useful for detecting synthetics, treatments, and place of origin. With emeralds, darkfield illumination can help you determine the depth of cracks, the type of filling present in fractures, and the extent to which an emerald may have been treated to hide cracks. In summary, darkfield lighting is a useful diagnostic aid, but it can be misleading when used for judging the clarity of colored stones.

Tips on Judging Clarity and Transparency

♦ **Clean the stone**. Otherwise, you may think dirt and spots are inclusions. Usually rubbing a stone with a lint-free cloth is sufficient. If you're examining jewelry at home, it may have to be cleaned with water. (See Chapter 12 for cleaning instructions.) Professional cleaning might also be necessary. Avoid touching the stone since fingers can leave smudges.

♦ **First examine the stone without magnification.** (However, if you require eyeglasses for reading, you'll need to wear them when examining gems.) Check if there are any noticeable flaws. If you are looking at a good tanzanite, you shouldn't see any. A good emerald, on the other hand, is likely to have eye-visible inclusions. However, the fewer flaws it has, the higher its value.

Check, too, the overall transparency of the stone. If your goal is to buy a high-quality emerald, avoid cloudy or opaque stones. Tanzanite should be very transparent.

♦ **Next, look at the stone under magnification.** This will help you spot threatening cracks that might go unnoticed with the unaided eye. Reliable jewelers will be happy to let you use their microscope or loupe (figure 6.13). If you're seriously interested in gemstones, you should own a fully-corrected, 10-power, triplet loupe. You can buy these at jewelry or gem supply stores. Plan on paying at least $25 for a good loupe. Cheaper types tend to distort objects.

People unaccustomed to loupes may find it easier to use a 5-power hand magnifier like the one by Bausch & Lomb in figure 6.13. Even though it does not show as much detail as a 10-power loupe, it has a broader viewing area and is particularly helpful for judging jewelry craftsmanship. You can buy one in optical shops and discount stores for about $7-$10. Be sure to specify **5-power**, otherwise they may sell you one that's only two power.

Fig. 6.13 A 10-power loupe resting on a 5-power hand magnifier.

♦ **Look at the stone from several angles**--top, bottom, sides. Even though top and centrally-located inclusions are the most undesirable in terms of beauty, those seen from the sides or bottom of a stone can affect its price or durability.

♦ **Look at the stone with light shining through it from the side** (transmitted light) or with darkfield illumination. This will help you see flaws inside the stone. It will also help you judge transparency, a key factor in determining the value of an emerald. Even when an emerald has good color and no eye-visible flaws, it won't have a high value if it's translucent or opaque. The emerald in figures 6.14 & 6.15 is an example of this. When viewed with the unaided eye under overhead lighting, the stone is a

Fig. 6.14 A translucent emerald in overhead lighting. The surface cracks are not noticeable to the unaided eye.

Fig. 6.15 Same stone viewed with darkfield illumination.

solid green color and has no noticeable inclusions or surface cracks. But it also has no life or sparkle. The fine particles of foreign material throughout the emerald reduce the light return from the facets. When light is shined through the stone from either the side or bottom, its translucency is obvious. The woman who bought this 1-carat stone paid $200 for it. This was a fair retail price, but it was no bargain.

♦ **Look at the stone with light reflected off the surface.** This will help you identify surface cracks. The central fracture across the emerald in figure 6.16 is visible but not prominent. However, when light is reflected off the stone's surface (fig 6.17), the crack is more obvious and you can easily see it's a surface-reaching crack rather than just an internal one. By then tilting the stone in transmitted light or darkfield illumination, you can determine that the crack is deep and serious. The presence of surface cracks in an emerald is a strong clue that the stone has probably been treated with an oil or epoxy filling to improve its appearance. The orange flashes visible in the fractures as the stone is moved suggest it has been filled with an epoxy substance.

Fig. 6.16 An emerald with a serious crack across it viewed in normal overhead lighting.

Fig. 6.17 When light is reflected off the surface of the stone, it is easier to see the crack and verify that it breaks the surface.

Fig. 6.18 In darkfield illumination, it's easier to locate the cracks and determine their length and depth. However, it's harder to tell if they reach the surface or are just internal. To judge fracture depth, the stone must be tilted.

Most emeralds with a good depth of color have surface cracks, and as a buyer you will need to make judgements about these cracks. Small, shallow fractures are not normally a problem, especially if they are on the bottom of the stone. However, a large, deep one could cause the stone to break in two when it is set or knocked accidently. Besides being a durability threat, large cracks or numerous ones can suggest a major change in appearance may have occurred when the emerald was treated with oil or epoxy. In other words, the clarity of the emerald could be a lot worse than what it appears to be.

The author took the 1-carat emerald in figures 6.16 to 6.18 to a Los Angeles dealer and asked him what he thought of it. His initial impression was the same as what the author's had been. It was a nice emerald, with decent color and a fair amount of life. Then he looked at it with a loupe. He changed his opinion very quickly. To him, this was a damaged stone which could break during setting. When asked what the stone would be worth, he said perhaps $350 a carat (wholesale); but he personally wouldn't buy the stone for that price because he'd have to disclose the crack to his customers and that would be a nuisance.

This emerald is a good example of why it's important to always examine stones under magnification before buying them. With the naked eye, serious cracks may not be visible, especially when a stone has a good depth of color.

♦ **When you judge clarity, compare stones of the same type**. Emeralds should be compared to emeralds, not to other gems, which typically have a higher clarity. Tanzanite, a very transparent, clean stone, should be compared to other tanzanites, not to sapphire, which tends to be more included.

♦ **Keep in mind that light-colored stones should have a better clarity than darker ones.** In lighter stones, inclusions are easier to see. Dark colors often mask flaws.

♦ **Remember that prongs and settings can hide flaws.** If you're interested in a stone with a high clarity, it may be best for you to buy a loose stone and have it set.

♦ **Keep in mind that your overall impression of a stone's clarity can be affected by the stones it is compared to.** A stone will look better when viewed next to one of low clarity than next to one of high clarity. To have a more balanced outlook, try to look at a variety of qualities.

Fig. 6.19

Top: **Fig. 6.20**. Bottom: **Fig. 6.21**

Do We Need Grades to Evaluate Clarity and Transparency?

The diamond industry has a standardized system for grading clarity based on a system developed by the GIA. Ten-power magnification is used. The advantage of having this system is that buyers can communicate what they want anywhere in the world. In addition, written appraisals and quality reports are more meaningful.

One of the drawbacks of the diamond grading system is that it has sometimes caused buyers to become so focused on color and clarity that they overlook brilliance and cut. Another drawback is that it has led people to judge stones by grades rather than with their eyes. No grade or lab report can give a full picture of what a stone looks like. In addition, grades are often misrepresented. Without examining a stone under magnification, one cannot tell if a grade has been inflated.

Even though clarity grading systems have been developed for colored stones, there is no one standardized system. In *The Ruby & Sapphire Buying Guide*, the author briefly presented the GIA and AGL clarity systems to help consumers understand appraisals and lab reports. Recently, she has learned there is a wide variation in how these grades are assigned by appraisers. The way transparency is incorporated into their systems differs. Therefore, it's best for you to ask your appraiser what his or her grades mean.

Grades are helpful for documentation purposes, but you don't need them to judge clarity and transparency. Look at the tanzanites in figures 6.19 to 6.21. Which do you think has the best clarity and which has the worst? If you chose figure 6.19 as the best and figure 6.21 as the worst, then you have just proved to yourself that you can make a clarity judgement without the aid of grades. Incidently, tanzanite dealers would consider the stone in figure 6.21 a reject and unsuitable for jewelry use.

Now look at the emeralds in figures 6.22 and 6.23. It's easy to tell that the stone in 6.23 is the most transparent. But it's debatable as to which one has the best clarity. Grades will not give you a good visual image of what these emeralds look like and how they differ. You have to examine the stones and form your own opinion of them. They look better to the naked eye than they do in these magnified photos. You can tell from the photos, though, that the stone in 6.23 has more life due to its higher transparency.

Fig. 6.22   **Fig. 6.23**

The term **life** has been mentioned three times in this chapter without being defined. It is frequently used by dealers to refer to the overall brilliance and sparkle of a gem. Some people equate it to "cut," but it's different because a stone can be well-cut yet have poor life. "Life" is not listed as a grading category on lab reports or appraisals, probably because it's difficult to define and quantify. Some of the factors that can influence your impression of "life" are:

Transparency. The higher the transparency the greater the life. This is a key factor in determining life in emerald. Emeralds without life commonly have a low transparency.

Faceting style. Brilliant- and mixed-cut stones generally have more life than step cuts. Step-cut emeralds can nevertheless look lively, but ones expectation of life in an emerald cut should be lower.

Proportions. Well-proportioned stones will return more light to the eye than poorly cut stones with "windows" (see chapter on judging cut). A gem can be well proportioned, though, and still lack life.

Polish. The higher the polish, the brighter a gem will look. Hard stones can take a higher polish than softer stones, so there are different expectations of polish luster depending on the gem species.

Clarity. Inclusions can impede light and brilliance, thereby lowering the life of a gem.

Amount of gray present Often the more grayish a stone is the duller it looks. This is one of the reasons grayish emeralds and tanzanite are less valued than stones with purer colors. Even gray diamonds can look dull, which is probably why at the wholesale level, they may cost less than yellowish diamonds of the same tone.

Tone. The lighter a stone is the more brilliant it can be. Keep in mind, though, that deep, saturated colors are a lot more highly valued than light colors.

No grade can convey how all of the above elements combine to give life and beauty to a stone. You need to have the visual experience of seeing the gem firsthand.

How Trade Opinions of Clarity and Transparency Can Differ

The way the clarity and transparency of a stone is perceived varies depending on who's examining it. In order to demonstrate this to you, the author showed two photographs (figs 6.24 & 6.25) to four different dealers. Then she asked them, "Assuming that the color and weight of these two emeralds are the same, which stone would you prefer?" The goal was to indirectly get them to comment on the clarity and transparency of the stones, but shape also became an issue.

Fig. 6.24 Emerald cut

Fig. 6.25 Marquise

The responses of the dealers are listed below along with the opinion of the author.

Dealer 1: "I like my stones clear. The marquise is a better stone because it has a better clarity and more life. In terms of shape, though, a marquise is the least valuable. It would be hard to find a buyer for it. People expect emeralds to have an emerald cut."

Dealer 2: "The emerald cut would be more salable because it's the expected shape for emeralds. Also, the inclusions are not as prominent (in the emerald cut) so there would be less resistance to it by a customer. The color will show more in the emerald cut. In colored stones, people look for color, not brilliance."

Dealer 3: "Perhaps the marquise. It has more life and is less included. The marquise shape usually costs more because it's more rare and gives a lower yield from the rough (than the emerald cut)."

Dealer 4: "I wouldn't carry either one in my inventory. The emerald cut is not even average--it's too included and too sleepy in the center. There's not much demand for the marquise. It's probably the least-valued shape for emeralds."

Author: Prefers the marquise because it's more transparent and has more life. Even though the outer ends of the emerald cut show some brilliance, the central focal part of the stone is dead. The marquise also has a pleasing shape outline and is a lot more distinctive than the usual emerald cut.

Despite their differences, each person above gave valid reasons for their choices. The photos of the two stones had previously been shown to an appraiser who has had a lot of experience evaluating colored gems. He described the clarity and transparency of the marquise as an HI_1 (heavily included) with moderate texture. He graded the emerald cut as as MI_2 to $\underline{HI_1}$ with moderate to strong texture (MI means moderately included). Another appraiser using the same grading system might have assigned different grades to the stones. But any knowledgeable appraiser or dealer would agree that neither of the emeralds is fine nor bottom quality. When compared to the stone in figure 6.26, the marquise and rectangular emerald cut look much better.

Fig. 6.26 Emerald with a poor clarity and poor transparency

There's a lot of subjectivity involved in grading and appraising gems. It doesn't matter which stone you think is best as long as you have good reasons for your choice. When buying gems, trust your own intuitions. Your opinion of a stone is just as important as your jeweler's.

7

Judging Tanzanite Color

It is Tanzanite's uncanny visual resemblance to the sapphire...that made a gemologist at Manhattan's Tiffany & Company hail its discovery as "the most exciting event of the century." Although it is actually a three-colored stone that shows flashes of purple and red, its predominant color is a deep royal blue. Since "blue is the most popular color in gems" according to Henry B. Platt, vice-president and director of Tiffany's and the man who gave Tanzanite its name, the potential market for the stone is huge.
Time, January 24, 1969.

Henry Platt did not underestimate the market potential for tanzanite. Today, some jewelry stores sell more tanzanite than sapphire. Though it used to be regarded as a sapphire substitute, tanzanite is now appreciated for its own unique qualities. Besides displaying flashes of purple or red, it may change color under different types of light.

How Lighting Affects Tanzanite Color

The color of all gems varies a little depending on the light source used. However, tanzanite often shows a distinct shift of color in different lighting. A tanzanite which appears blue or violet in daylight or fluorescent lighting may look purple under **incandescent** (ordinary bulb) light. Some people prefer a strong change of color. Others place a higher value on stones which are blue in both fluorescent and indoor incandescent lighting. The following chart indicates how different lighting may affect tanzanite color. Not all tanzanite changes color. However, most of the tanzanites photographed for this book did show a distinct shift of color.

Type of Lighting	Effect of Lighting on Tanzanite
Sunlight	At midday, it normally has a neutral effect on the hue. Earlier and later in the day, it adds red, orange, or yellow making stones look more purplish.
Light bulbs and candlelight	Add red. Purple colors are strengthened, blue may turn violet or purple, and grayish colors may look brownish. The degree of change varies depending on the stone. Some stones show little change.
Fluorescent lights	Depends on what type they are. Most strengthen the blue in tanzanite.
Halogen spotlights	Add sparkle and usually make stones look more purple. The color change is generally less than with light bulbs.
Light under an overcast sky	Adds blue and gray

The whitest, most neutral light is at midday. Besides adding the least amount of color, this light makes it easier to see the various nuances of color. Consequently, gemologists like to use daylight-equivalent lighting when grading stones. Neutral fluorescent bulbs approximate this ideal, but some of these lights are better than others. Three that are recommended for colored-stone grading are the Duro-Test Vita Lite, the GE Chroma 50 and Sylvania Design 50.

Since tanzanite can change color, it should also be evaluated under an incandescent lamp (a pen-light is not a large enough light source). If a written appraisal is being done on the stone, the color under both fluorescent and incandescent light should be noted. Your final judgement of a tanzanite and any gemstone, however, should be based on its appearance in daylight equivalent light.

Judging Tanzanite Color

Tanzanite can display different colors even under a single light source. When you look at it from one angle, it may be purple or lavender. From another angle it can look more blue. From other angles, you may see various combinations of blue, violet, and purple. Therefore, the orientation of a tanzanite is very important in determining its face-up color.

Fig. 7.1 A high-quality, medium-dark tanzanite viewed in daylight equivalent light

Fig. 7.2 Same tanzanite lit with light-bulbs

Fig. 7.3 Medium-light tanzanite under fluorescent lighting

Fig. 7.4 Under incandescent lighting, the stone resembles an amethyst.

Fig. 7.5 A slightly grayish tanzanite in daylight equivalent lighting

Fig. 7.6 The same stone is slightly brownish under incandescent light.

Note: The actual colors of these stones may be a little different than shown. The printing and developing processes usually alter the true color of gems in photographs.

There are some differences of opinion as to what is the best face-up **hue** for a tanzanite. According to tanzanite dealer Abe Suleman, "It has long been accepted that a true blue tanzanite with a faint purple secondary color has been the most desirable. This is because the stone was first considered as a sapphire substitute. Also, blue stones whatever they are, when used for jewelry, inevitably will be considered and compared against sapphire. Today, blue sapphire still reigns as the desired stone, whether in a Ceylon, Burma or Kashmir blue. Therefore, the true blue tanzanite will always fetch a premium over purplish stones."

Gem-dealer William Larson says he'll pay more for blue but prefers purple because he likes stones that look significantly different from sapphire. Dealer Cynthia Marcusson feels there is too much emphasis placed on the high value of sapphire-blue stones. She states, "While the pure blues can fetch a high price, fine color mix gems can be priced as high and I find they are preferred by the consumer. The unique mix of colors in tanzanite allows it to be all it can be: exotic, rare and unlike any other gem, and this attitude is backed up by the consumer."

Sellers who prefer blue with a **strong** purple secondary color may not put any premiums on very blue stones. However, when tanzanites are purple under both incandescent and fluorescent lighting, they generally sell for less, no matter who is selling them. The main reason for this is there's a greater demand for stones that look like sapphire rather than amethyst.

Even though hues ranging from blue to violetish blue command the highest prices, other tanzanite colors are also appreciated. Some jewelry designers use tanzanite in their pieces specifically because it offers them exotic shades of purple and "lilac" not found in other gems.

The most valued tanzanite **tones** range from medium-dark to dark. Light tones are the least expensive. Stones with medium tones are often the most colorful because they have fewer black extinction areas than darker stones and a stronger color than lighter ones. There is a direct correlation between the depth of color and the carat weight of the stone. Medium-dark tones of tanzanite can be hard to find in stones weighing less than 2 carats. In tanzanite, larger sizes usually permit a greater concentration of color. Consequently, it's not easy for a 2-carat tanzanite to compete in color with a 10-carat stone. Emerald, on the other hand, is more likely to have a good depth of color in small sizes. A **1/10** carat Sandawana emerald, for example, is typically more saturated in color than a **1**-carat tanzanite.

Even though the most valuable tanzanites have a good depth of color, they should not be so dark that they look like black onyx. The purpose of buying tanzanite is to see color not black.

Fig. 7.7 21.88-ct multi-colored tanzanite with three distinct color zones. The gem was cut in cabochon to allow each color to show distinctly without the mixing of colors that would occur with a faceted pavilion. *Photo courtesy Cynthia Renée Co.; photography by Weldon.*

Fig. 7.8 From another angle, the same multi-colored tanzanite is purple and yellowish. *Photo courtesy Cynthia Renée Co.; photography by Weldon.*

Fig. 7.9 An example of the attractive mixture of colors seen in some tanzanites. Don't expect to find other tanzanites with the exact same coloration pattern.

Fig. 7.10 The stones in these two earrings are not an exact match but they blend together well. Finding matched tanzanites is a challenge. *Photo courtesy Cynthia Renée Co.; photography by Weldon.*

Color purity is just as important in tanzanite as it is in emerald. The grayer or browner a stone is, the less it is valued. Pure colors are the most prized.

If you plan to buy tanzanite earrings or a piece with more than one tanzanite, keep in mind that tanzanite is hard to match. This is because it is a combination of three hues which may blend together or show up as flashes of different color. In gemology texts, tanzanite is classified as a **trichroic** (three-color) gem. Blue and purple (lavender in light tones) are usually two of the colors. The third color, which may not be visible, can be green, yellow, orange, red or brown or a mixture of any of these colors. Due to all the possible variations of color, it can be hard to find matching stones. Abe Suleman estimates that in a parcel of 2,000 carats of tanzanite, he may only be able to find one or two matched pairs of stones. When dealers need matched pairs, they are usually forced to cut the pairs from the same piece of rough and often have to sacrifice yields to acquire the matches. Even in cutting from the same piece of rough, if a slight mistake is made in the orientation of the stones, the color can perceptively vary.

The differing degrees of color change in tanzanite add to the difficulty of matching stones. Two stones that look alike under a cool white fluorescent tube may not match under a warm white tube. Under incandescent light, there may be an even greater difference between the two stones. As a result, when matching tanzanite, greater leniency is required than with other gems. The most one can reasonably expect from a tanzanite piece is that the stones blend together well.

When evaluating tanzanite color, pay close attention to the lighting in the store, and try to examine the stones under various light sources. As mentioned earlier, fluorescent lighting usually emphasizes the blue whereas halogen spotlights tend to highlight the purple in the stone. Your impression of tanzanite color will be greatly affected by the surrounding light.

Three Common Beliefs Which Warrant Review

♦ **Color is the most important factor for valuing colored stones**. Color is a major value factor, but it's not always the most important one. Suppose you have a fine $10,000-a-carat emerald. If it were translucent with the exact same color, it would be worth several times less, and transparency would be the main factor contributing to its lower value. Fractures in tanzanite can have a significant effect both on its price and salability. On the other hand, light purple colors can be very desirable even though they're priced lower than deep blues. If you examined the reject stones of colored stone dealers, you'd find that most of the stones were rejected because of poor clarity and/or transparency. This doesn't mean clarity is more important than color. It just indicates that the importance of each price factor varies from one stone to another. Consumers who focus on color and play down other value factors risk getting a poor buy. When buying colored gems, remember--color is not everything, even though it does play a substantial role.

♦ **Color is just a matter of individual preference.** This is a common answer to the question, "What is the most valuable color?" The erroneous implication is that there are no trade standards for preferred colors. Emerald and tanzanite pricing is based on some universal principles regarding gem color--the less brown or gray present and the more saturated the color, the more valuable the stone. For each stone, there is also a range of hues which command a higher price than others. Even though your choice of color should be determined by what you like, you need to know how color is valued in order to accurately compare prices.

♦ **Dealers evaluate their stones in a logical, analytical manner.** Dealers tend to evaluate gem quality as a whole rather than breaking it down to its constituent parts of clarity, transparency, proportions, etc. Their final judgments are usually more intuitive than logical. In addition, non-quality-related factors also enter into their pricing of gems. Some of these price determinants are demand, form of payment, buyer's credit rating, amount purchased, and competitors' prices. Often you can find the same dealer selling a stone of higher quality for less than one of lower quality. This is because the rough for the higher quality stone may have cost less. Or, the rate of currency exchange could have been more favorable at the time of purchase. Therefore, you should not assume that higher price necessarily means higher quality. Conversely, lower price is not necessarily indicative of a deal.

Since you can't always count on prices to reflect the quality of gems, it's all the more important that you learn to make quality judgments yourself. The reason this book analyzes color and gem quality in terms of their component parts is to aid you in this process. Vague statements such as "look for color" or "grass green is best" are not very helpful to consumers. However, when you learn how the color elements of hue, tone and color purity affect the price of a gem, it's easier for you to understand gem valuation. Your ultimate goal should be to reach the level where you can make quick global judgments about gem quality. But like any other skill, this takes practice.

What Color Emerald or Tanzanite is Best for You?

To answer this question, consider the following factors:

♦ **Your purpose for buying the stone.** If you're buying a stone just for personal pleasure, it doesn't matter which color you choose as long as it looks good on you. But if you plan to resell it later, you would probably be better off to avoid grayish and brownish colors and stones with very light tones.

♦ **Your budget.** Color has a major effect on the price of stones. A medium-dark, pure color emerald or tanzanite may not fit your budget, but a slightly different color could be in your price-range. Price is determined by color, clarity, transparency, cut, and size. Play with these factors to determine what you want for your budget.

♦ **The availability of the color**. If you're looking for an emerald with a high color saturation and money is no object, you still may have a hard time finding it in the size and quality you want. If you're serious about the stone, your jeweler can call around to various dealers to try to find you one. In the end, though, you may have to compromise on either the color, quality, or size, or wait until the desired stone can be found.

♦ **Your wardrobe**. If you buy jewelry that blends with your existing wardrobe, you'll be able to wear the jewelry more often.

♦ **Your personal preference and personality**. This should play a major role in your choice. Instinctively, you often prefer what looks best on you. According to color psychologists, there can also be a link between your personality and your color preferences.

Sometimes, we expect jewelry salespeople to tell us what color is best for us. They can guide us in our choices, but in the end, we need to consider all of the above factors and then make the final decision ourselves when buying gems for our personal pleasure. If we do, we should end up with stones that will not only enhance our appearance but that can also bring us long-term enjoyment.

8

Judging Cut

Cut plays a major role in determining the value of emeralds and tanzanites because it affects their color and clarity as well as their brilliance. For example, a stone that is cut too shallow can look pale and lifeless, and it can display flaws that would normally not be visible to the naked eye.

The term **cut** is sometimes confusing because it has a variety of meanings. Jewelers use it to refer to:

♦ The **shape** of a gemstone (e.g. round or oval)

♦ The **cutting style** (e.g. cabochon or faceted, brilliant or step cut, single or full cut)

♦ The **proportions** of a stone (e.g. pavilion depth, girdle thickness)

♦ The **finish** of a stone (e.g. polishing marks or smooth flawless surface, misshapen or symmetrical facets)

The proportions and finish are also called the **make** of the stone. Proportions and how they affect the appearance of emeralds and tanzanites will be the focus of this chapter. Shape and cutting style were discussed in Chapter Four. Finish will not be discussed because it normally does not have much of an effect on the price of colored stones. If there is a problem with the finish, it can usually be corrected by repolishing the stone. Blemishes such as scratches and abrasions are sometimes considered as part of the finish grade of the stone. This book classifies them as clarity elements.

Judging the Face-up View

Colored stones should display maximum color. However, if they are cut with improper angles, their color potential can be diminished with what is called a **window**--a washed out area which allows you to see right through the stone. Windows (or windowing) can occur in any transparent, faceted stone no matter how light or dark it is and no matter how deep or shallow its pavilion is. The larger the window, the poorer the cut is.

To look for windows, hold the stone about an inch or two (2 to 5 cm) above a contrasting background such as your hand or a piece of white paper. Then try to look straight through the top of the stone **without tilting it**, and check if you can see the background or a light window-like area in the center of it. If the stone is light colored, you might try holding it above a printed page to see if the print shows through.

Fig. 8.1 A moderate window in a tanzanite   **Fig. 8.2** Print visible through a large window

When evaluating a stone for windowing, you will probably notice dark areas in it. The GIA refers to these as extinction areas or simply **extinction**. All transparent faceted gems have some dark areas. However, a good cut can reduce extinction and increase color. One should expect dark stones to have a higher percentage of dark areas than those which are lighter colored. You should also expect there to be more extinction than what you see in pictures of gems. During shooting, photographers normally use two or more front lights to make stones show as much color as possible. When you look at a stone, you will usually be using a single light source, so less color and more black will show. The broader and more diffused the light is, the more colorful the stone will look. Therefore, compare stones under the same type and amount of lighting.

Fig. 8.3 This tanzanite displays a lot of color even though it was lit with just one front light. It weighs almost 21 carats and has a checkerboard-cut faceting style.

Fig. 8.4 Three front lights were used when photographing this 11-carat tanzanite. It has an unusually good depth of color.

Both of the stones in figures 8.3 and 8.4 are well-cut and have the same wholesale price, but they each have different advantages. The cushion-shape tanzanite is more colorful particularly when viewed outdoors or under more lights. The trilliant, though, has a better depth of color. Either stone would be ideal for a jewelry piece. The final choice should depend on individual preference.

The quality and complexity of the faceting should also be considered when judging cut. Note the intricate faceting patterns of all the stones on this page. They were all fashioned by highly skilled cutters in Idar-Oberstein, Germany. A premium is charged for this type of cutting whether it be done in Germany or some other country. Compare these stones to the ones with windowing on the previous page and you'll see how a high quality cut can improve the appearance of a stone. The faceting of emeralds is usually less precise and less complex because the cost of the rough is greater. Finding an emerald without windowing can be difficult. Nevertheless, emeralds can be well-cut and display good color and brilliance.

Fig. 8.5 Note the intricate faceting patterns on this 4.50-carat tanzanite.

Fig. 8.6 An 11-carat tanzanite featuring Idar-style cutting. *Photo courtesy Cynthia Renée Co.; photography by Weldon.*

When you hear the term **brilliance** used, keep in mind that it has different definitions. In the GIA Colored Stone Grading Course, it is defined as the percentage of light return in a gem after the percentage of windowing and extinction are subtracted. AGL (American Gemological Laboratories) uses "brilliance" only in connection with the amount of windowing present. A stone with no window whatsoever would receive a brilliance grade of 100%. This high of a brilliance percentage would not be possible under the GIA system because there is always some extinction present in transparent faceted gems. In this book, the term "brilliant" is used in the colloquial sense of having both a high intensity and large area of light return. A dull-looking, low-transparency stone with no window would not described as "brilliant" under this non-technical definition.

Another thing to notice when judging the face-up view is the outline of the shape. If it's a standard shape that should be symmetrical, check if it is. If you plan to resell the stone later on, make sure it's a shape others might like. A very long skinny marquise or emerald cut, for example, may be hard to sell. With emerald, conserving weight from the rough is often more of a priority than good symmetry.

Judging the Profile

When you buy an emerald or tanzanite, be sure to look at its profile. The side view can indicate:

♦ If the stone is suitable for mounting in jewelry.

♦ If the stone will look big or small for its weight.

♦ If the cutter's main goal was to bring out the stone's brilliance.

When evaluating the profile, hold the stone widthwise and **check the overall depth** (referred to in the trade as the **total depth percentage**). If you look at it lengthwise, the stone could look too shallow when in fact it may have an adequate depth. You should expect well-cut colored stones to be deeper than diamonds, which have a high refractive index (a measure of the degree to which light is bent as it travels through a gem).

Noted mineralogist John Sinkankas makes this point in his book, *Emerald and Other Beryls* (page 334). He writes, "In the case of higher refractive index gemstones, inner reflections can result from shallower bottom angles, thus allowing these gems to be cut less deeply. This becomes apparent when two brilliant gems of the same size and style of cutting are compared, one being diamond and the other a beryl. It will be seen that the diamond is cut to less depth while the beryl had to be cut to greater depth in order to insure upward reflection of light."

Fig. 8.7 Profile of a well-cut tanzanite

Fig. 8.8 Face-up view of same tanzanite

Fig. 8.9 This stone is not deep enough to prevent windowing. However, it has better symmetry than many emeralds.

Fig. 8.10 Same emerald viewed face-up. Note the window in the center of the stone.

Fig. 8.11 Emerald with an acceptable total depth. In relation to the pavilion, though, the crown is too shallow.

Fig. 8.12 Hardly any window is present in this emerald. If this stone were transparent, it would show a high degree of brilliance.

Figure 8.13 serves as an example of a colored stone with a good overall depth while reviewing some fundamental gem terminology.

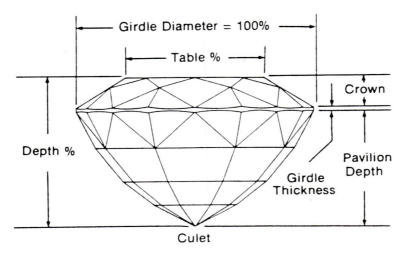

Proportions: Cutting

Fig. 8.13 Profile diagram of a mixed-cut colored stone. *Copyright by American Gemological Laboratories, Inc., 1978.*

The **total depth percentage** of the stone in figure 8.13 can be calculated as follows:

depth
width (girdle diameter)

In this case, the total depth percentage is 65%, which is a good depth/width ratio for a colored stone. There are differences of opinion as to what is the best depth percentage for an emerald or tanzanite. Some say 60 to 65%. Others say 65 to 80%. Combining these two ranges, we can conclude that a stone's depth should range between 60 to 80% of its width.

If a stone is much deeper when you look at it widthwise, then it may not be suitable for mounting in jewelry and it will look small for its weight in the face-up view. The main reason for cutting extremely deep stones is to save as much weight from the original rough as possible. Stones may also be cut deep to darken their color, especially if they are pale or color-zoned. Unnecessary weight adds to the cost of the stone since prices are calculated by multiplying the weight times the per-carat cost. Consequently, when you compare the prices of stones, you should consider their overall depth.

If a stone is extremely shallow ("flat") when you look at it widthwise, it might be fragile and therefore unsuitable as a stone for an everyday ring (it could, however, be good for a pendant, brooch or earrings). Very shallow stones look big for their weight in the face-up view, but unfortunately they often have big windows and lack life, which brings down their value. The main reason for cutting extremely shallow stones is to save as much weight from the original rough as possible. Stones may also be cut shallow to lighten their color.

When judging the profile of an emerald or tanzanite, you should also **pay attention to the crown height and the pavilion depth**. Notice the relationship of the crown height to the pavilion depth in the diagram of figure 8.7 (about 3.5 to 1). Then compare the profile views in this chapter to the diagram. Without even measuring these stones, you can make visual judgments about their pavilion and crown heights.

If the crown is too low, the stone will lack sparkle. When light falls on a flat crown, there tends to be a large sheet-like reflection off the table facet instead of twinkles of light from the other crown facets.

If the crown or pavilion is too flat or too deep, the stone may lack life, have a window, or look blackish. In order for the stone to effectively reflect light, the crown and especially the pavilion must be angled properly. But they can't have the proper angles if they don't have the proper depth.

While evaluating the profile, look at the curvature of the **pavilion outline**. A very lumpy, **bulging pavilion** decreases brilliance and helps create dark or window-like areas in the stone. This is because the pavilion is not slanted at an angle that will maximize light reflection. A bulging pavilion is not uncommon in emerald, and it is another example of how you can end up paying for excess weight that only reduces the beauty of the stone. Unlike diamonds, colored stones should have a slight pavilion curvature. This helps decrease windowing as the stone is tilted.

Notice, too, the **symmetry** of the profile. Symmetry problems such as an **off-center culet** prevent light from reflecting evenly. (In cushions, ovals, and marquises, the culet should be centered widthwise and lengthwise. In hearts and pear-shapes, the culet should only be centered widthwise.) It's common for emeralds to look less symmetrical than stones such as diamonds and tanzanites. However, when emeralds are so lopsided that their brilliance is seriously diminished, the lack of symmetry is unacceptable.

Fig. 8.14 Emerald with an off-center culet and a crown that is too thin.

Fig. 8.15 The thick girdle will make this tanzanite look small for its weight face-up.

Fig. 8.16 Tanzanite with a crown that is too high, a pavilion that is much too shallow, and an uneven girdle that's too thick.

Fig. 8.17 This emerald has a crown that is too low, a pavilion that is a little too bulgy, and a slightly off-center culet.

Fig. 8.18 Example of low-quality cutting on a poor-quality emerald with no transparency.

Also check the **girdle width**. Stones with very thin girdles are hard to set and easy to chip. Stones with thick girdles have reduced brilliance, look smaller than they weigh, and are also hard to set. The judgment of girdle thickness is best done with the eye, with and without magnification. If the girdle looks like a wide band encircling the stone, it's probably too thick. If the girdle is sharp and you can hardly see it, then it's probably too thin. **Wavy and uneven girdles** can also create setting problems. In addition, they indicate that the cutter did not pay much attention to detail.

How Cut Affects Price

Theoretically, major cutting defects should reduce emerald and tanzanite prices substantially. In actual practice, this is not always true.

Sometimes the cut may have no direct effect on the per-carat price. For example a 1/2-carat tanzanite pendant may be mass-produced and sold at the same price in chain stores. Some of the tanzanites may be well-cut. Others of similar color and clarity may have large windows. In spite of their identical price, the value of the better-cut tanzanites should be greater.

In some stores, you can select an emerald or tanzanite from an assortment of stones in a packet or little bowl. The per-carat price for all the stones may be the same even though they might vary considerably in quality. People who know how to judge cut, color, clarity, and transparency will get the best buys in cases like these because they will be able to pick out the most valuable stones and avoid paying for unnecessary weight.

Sometimes the cut has a mathematically calculated effect on the price of gems. For example, the prices of fine-quality princess cuts that are calibrated to specific millimeter sizes may be determined by the weight lost when cutting the stones.

If you were to have a large stone recut to bring out its brilliance, you could calculate its new per-carat price by dividing the new weight into the combined cost of the recutting and the stone.

The increased value of a stone after recutting can more than make up for its lost weight and cutting costs. Consequently, it is not uncommon for fine-quality gem material to be recut to improve the proportions. There are risks, however, to recutting gems. Their value may decrease due to breakage or color lightening.

Sometimes the cut affects prices in a subjective manner. Some dealers place a greater importance on cut than others, and they may discount a very poorly cut stone as much as 50% in order to sell it. Another dealer might discount the same stone 25%.

Premiums of between 10 to 25% may be added to precision-cut tanzanite, such as those in figures 8.3 to 8.6. But considering the fact that fine-cut stones don't have unnecessary weight, their total cost may not be much more than that of a bulky stone with the same face-up size.

There is no established trade formula for determining percentage-wise how cut affects the value of emerald or tanzanite. There is, however, agreement that a well-proportioned, brilliant stone is more valuable than one which is poorly cut. As you shop, you may discover that well-cut stones are not always readily available, particularly in the case of emerald. This is unfortunate because man has control over a stone's cut. There could be a better selection of well-cut emeralds, but the public has to ask for this.

9

Treatments

Emerald dealers are faced with a real dilemma. They sell a stone that, in its natural state, normally has lots of eye-visible flaws. Their customers, however, want stones that look clean to the naked eye.

Tanzanite dealers do not have this problem. Most of their stones are eye-clean and highly transparent. Tanzanite, though, often has an undesirable color in its original state. This chapter will discuss what emerald and tanzanite dealers have done to enhance the color and clarity of their stones.

Heat Treatment

When mined, tanzanite often looks brownish or grayish with tinges of purple or blue. A more attractive blue/purple color can result if the material is slowly heated to 600-700 degrees centigrade. This process must be closely monitored because rapid changes in temperature can fracture tanzanite as it will any other stone. The heat treatment is normally done after cutting as the stones have to be clean or damage will occur when heated. The color change is permanent, so no fading will occur. It's estimated that between 95 to 99% of the violetish-blue tanzanite on the market today has been heated. (Heat treatment, by the way, should only be done by professionals. Damage to the tanzanite or injuries to people can result if done by amateurs).

Tanzanite crystals are found in a variety of other colors besides brown and gray. Some tanzanite crystals are blue and purple when mined (fig. 9.2). Most of these are heated to intensify their color, but a few require no treatment. Other crystals might look yellow, green, pink, orange or red before heat treatment. Tanzanite dealer Abe Suleman says that "The color intensity of treated tanzanite is commensurate to the intensity of the

Fig. 9.1 Four color varieties of zoisite (tanzanite) viewed under incandescent lighting (light-bulbs). The purplish stone on the right was heat treated. Before the treatment, it may have been grayish or yellowish like the two center stones, or another color.

Fig. 9.2 A faceted tanzanite flanked by two unheated and unpolished tanzanite crystals. Some tanzanite is blue and purple before heat treatment. Heating can intensify the color.

blues, purples, and brown before it was cooked. Yellowish and greenish colors in the rough don't always produce the best stones. Green, for example, may produce the steely blue color, and the yellow, a grayish stone."

The price of tanzanite stones is based on their final color, not the color prior to heating. There's generally no price difference between treated and untreated tanzanite.

The heat treatment of tanzanite is a fully accepted practice within the trade. All of the tanzanite dealers the author questioned at gem shows and in offices readily acknowledged that their stones were heat treated. A few even used heat treatment as a selling point. One seller pointed out how amazing it was that an unattractive tanzanite could become a "beautiful swan" in the world of gemstones through a simple heating process. The willingness of tanzanite dealers to disclose heat treatment is good evidence that it is well accepted by the trade.

Fracture Filling

Most emeralds have small surface-reaching cracks. If they are filled with an appropriate oil, the fractures are less noticeable and the overall color may improve. Unfortunately, oil can evaporate over time and sometimes may leave a white or brown residue. This is not a major problem because the stone can be cleaned out by repeated immersion in a solvent such as lacquer thinner. Afterwards it can be re-oiled to look as good as when it was bought.

Emerald treaters have been trying to develop fillings which are more permanent. During the past five years they have experimented with epoxy glues or resins. Sometimes these are referred to as **Opticon** because that's the brand name of one of the best known epoxy resins. Epoxy fillers evaporate more slowly than oil and hide the flaws better. Hardeners (also called plasticizers or stabilizers) may be added to help seal in the fillings and make them more permanent. Emeralds treated with fillers containing hardeners are said to be **stabilized**.

Originally, epoxy resin fillings promised to be a better alternative to oiling. Now, however, many dealers consider them unacceptable, particularly for higher quality emeralds. Like oil, an epoxy can over a period of years dry out, turn whitish, and lose its ability to mask flaws. (High quality epoxies tend to last better than the cheaper types.) If a hardener has been added to the epoxy, it may be difficult or impossible to extract all of the filling and retreat the emerald properly. Therefore, epoxy treatments may not be reversible in the way emerald oiling is. Curiously, non-permanent oils have turned out to be the preferred fillers for good quality emeralds.

Other types of fillers are also being developed, but oiling is the emerald treatment jewelers and dealers are most comfortable with. Many trade members are reluctant to accept new fillers when their long-term effects are not known.

Colorless oils and resins often enhance the color of an emerald by making it appear more transparent and less milky. Occasionally, green dye is added to a filler to further improve on the color. Most trade members consider the use of colored fillers an unacceptable practice, especially if it's not disclosed. Nevertheless, you should suspect colored oil or epoxy whenever you see bargain-priced emeralds with an intense green color.

Detecting and Identifying Emerald Fillings

Emeralds must have cracks in order to be fracture-filled, and the cracks must reach the surface of the stone at some point. Otherwise a filling cannot be introduced into the stone. Therefore, to detect fillings in emeralds, you should look for breaks on their surface. Sometimes these are visible with the naked eye. But usually magnification is needed. When light is reflected onto the stone, the surface fractures are easier to spot.

If an emerald has surface cracks, it has probably been **clarity enhanced** (fracture-filled to improve its clarity). If the cracks are numerous or large, the change in clarity could be significant. Keep in mind that fillers are used to either de-emphasize or hide fractures. Consequently, filled fractures are sometimes very hard to locate. The stone should be viewed through a microscope from many different angles using darkfield and reflected light. Laypeople need professional assistance.

Gemologists and dealers use a variety of clues to identify emerald fillings and determine their impact on the clarity. Some are:

♦ **Orange or yellow color flashes in the fractures** as the stone is rocked back and forth (fig. 9.4). In some emeralds, the orange alternates to a blue flash. This orange/yellow and orange/yellow-to-blue flash effect is commonly seen in stones treated with Opticon, especially if a hardener has been added. It is not a characteristic of oiled stones.
   The color flashes in emeralds are most easily seen under a microscope, but they are often visible through a 10-power hand magnifier. Keep in mind that the color flashes must be along the fractures. Non-treated stones will show blue and orange/-yellow flashes off the facets but not along the cracks. Epoxy-treated stones do not always display orange/yellow or blue color flashes along breaks.

♦ **Residue and air bubbles** (figs. 9.3 & 9.5). These can be found in oil- and epoxy-filled fractures. Inexperienced viewers might mistake natural emerald inclusions for filling residue and vice versa.

Fig. 9.3 Residue and trapped air bubbles in a fracture of an epoxy-filled emerald. *Photo courtesy AIGS (Asian Institute of Gemological Sciences); photo by Gary Du Toit.*

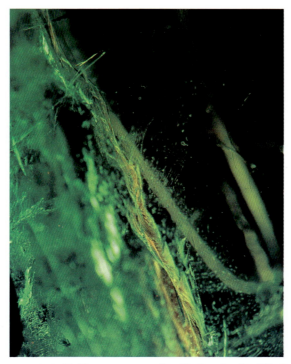

Fig. 9.4 Yellow-orange color flashes in the filled fractures of an epoxy-treated emerald. When these emeralds are tilted so the background becomes lighter, the flashes may disappear or turn blue. *Photo courtesy AIGS; photo by Gary Du Toit.*

Fig. 9.5 The oil in this emerald has evaporated and left a residue. The stone needs to be re-oiled.

◆ **Ultraviolet fluorescence**. Many oil fillings show a yellowish-green to greenish-yellow fluorescence under long-wave ultraviolet light. Epoxy fillings don't. Keep in mind that fluorescence is merely an indication. Some stones with oil don't fluoresce. Stones filled with both oil and epoxy can display the same fluorescence as those treated only with oil.

◆ **Thermal reaction**. When a hot needle is put next to a fracture opening, oil will "sweat" and form beads along the edge of the fracture. An epoxy sealed at the surface with a hardener does not do this. However, movement of the epoxy in the fractures may be visible under magnification. This thermal test should only be performed by professionals because if it's not done properly, the hot needle can cause the stone to crack or shatter.

◆ **Reaction to immersion in solvents**. Some dealers place emeralds in acetone or alcohol to determine the extent and type of filling. Most oils dissolve in acetone whereas hardened epoxy doesn't. Evidence of filler removal can be seen under magnification. Stronger solvents such as methylene chloride are used to dissolve epoxy fillings.

   Some jewelers spot-check their emerald jewelry for colored oils by placing it in a solvent. If the color of the emerald(s) becomes a lot lighter, the jewelers know a colored filler has been used, and they return the merchandise.

   Laypeople and appraisers should not use solvents to test an emerald. The emerald will probably look less attractive if the filling is dissolved. Afterwards, they'll have to pay to get it professionally re-oiled. For best results, emerald oiling should be done with special oils and sophisticated vacuum processes. Simple immersion in the proper oils sometimes works, but it doesn't always restore the emerald to its original filled state.

   More detailed information on identifying emerald fillings is available in the two following articles:
   "Identification of fissure-treated gemstones" by Dr. H. A. Hanni, *Journal of Gemology*, October 1992, pp. 201-205.
   "Fracture Filling of Emeralds, Opticon and Traditional 'Oils'" *Gems & Gemology*, Summer 1991, pp 70-85.

Disclosing Treatments

   Many jewelry professionals believe it's acceptable to treat emeralds as long as the treatment is disclosed. As gemologist Michael van Moppes writes in "Letters to the editors" of *Gem & Jewellery News* (Sep. 1993 pg 62), "Stones are treated for one of two reasons: to improve or to deceive. The only difference between these is disclosure. A treatment which is disclosed is an honest attempt to improve on nature: the consumer is free to decide whether the improvement is acceptable. A treatment which is not disclosed is an attempt to trick the buyer into believing the stone is better than it naturally is."

Some sellers think the gem trade is making a big mistake by disclosing treatments. They're worried that people won't want to buy gems if they know how they are enhanced. These sellers also feel that if their competitors aren't informing customers of treatments, they shouldn't have to either.

Other trade members believe that it's pointless to disclose emerald oiling because it's a standard trade practice. However, they may feel that other types of treatments warrant disclosure. In an article in *Gem & Jewellery News* (June 1994 pg 35), Harry Levy states, "There are no emeralds which have not been oiled in the cutting and polishing process. And nature has devised it so that practically every emerald retains some of this oil. There is no point in declaring a process that is universally used. All leathers are tanned, that is how we turn hide into leather, but no one talks of oiled leather." Later in his article, Mr. Levy lists some drawbacks of accepting epoxies such as Opticon as a standard emerald treatment and points out the complexities of establishing disclosure regulations.

Some people think all fillers other than oils should be banned from use in emeralds, rather than just disclosed. In their opinion, these fillings are too difficult to detect and they are complicating the emerald business.

The US Federal Trade Commission requires that gem enhancements be disclosed. In cases where the treatment(s) can't be identified, salespeople are supposed to make a general statement such as "Most emeralds are treated with substances like oil to improve their clarity." Some of the organizations in America that urge their members to follow the guidelines of the commission are:

AGA (Accredited Gemologists Association)
AGTA (The American Gem Trade Organization)
ASA (American Society of Appraisers)
AGS (American Gem Society)
ISA (International Society of Appraisers)
Jewelers of America
NAJA (National Association of Jewelry Appraisers)

Organizations outside the US have also adopted disclosure policies regarding gem enhancements. All of these organizations believe it's important for the jewelry industry to develop the trust of the public.

Disclosure laws are not unique to the jewelry industry. In California, real estate agents must disclose any negative details such as electrical and plumbing problems, earthquake and termite damage, toxic dumps or noise in the neighborhood, etc. As in all businesses, there are some sellers who don't comply with the law, but they risk being sued and losing their licenses. On the other hand, agents who disclose all pertinent information find their business increases due to referrals from satisfied clients.

General disclosure information can be just as important as specific data. When a jewelry salesperson forewarns customers of routine treatments like emerald oiling, this prevents an unpleasant surprise when they take their emerald piece to another store to be cleaned or repaired and are told the emerald is treated. It also helps customers understand why emeralds need special care.

Enhancement terminology can be misleading. Terms such as "stabilized" and "enhanced" may lead you to believe that a treatment is stable and completely positive when it isn't. Sometimes the definition of "treatment" is changed so that it excludes routine treatments like emerald oiling.

In this book **treatment** refers to any process such as heating, oiling, stabilizing, waxing, dying, bleaching, and irradiation which alters the color or clarity of a gem. Enhancement is used as an alternate term, but it has a broader meaning. Enhancement may also refer to the faceting and polishing of a gem.

What Salespeople Should Be Able to Tell You about Emerald Treatments

Salespeople should not be expected to know how to identify the fillers in emeralds. Even the world's foremost gem laboratories find this difficult. Often, more than one substance is used as a filler. Some of the filling materials are new, and conclusive detection methods have not been developed for them. The science of identifying emerald enhancements is in its initial stages.

Salespeople should know, however, that emeralds are usually treated with oil or other fillers to improve their clarity, and they should tell you this. They should also be able to explain to you why emeralds need special attention and how you should care for them.

Clothing manufacturers can sew written instructions into their products. They'll say, for example, "dry clean only," "no bleach," "cool iron," "do not wring or twist," etc. It's not possible to place this kind of information on gems. Therefore, it's the salesperson's responsibility to tell you how to look after your jewelry purchases.

Salespeople should warn you, for example, not to soak your emerald jewelry in warm soapy water because detergents may wash out some of the oil, making the flaws more visible. They should also tell you to keep your emerald away from hot lights, the sun, and any other source of heat because they can make the filler dry out more quickly. Therefore, it's not advisable to wear emerald jewelry to the beach or leave it sitting on a window sill.

In summary, you should be able to get practical advice and basic facts about gem treatments from salespeople. For technical information about a specific emerald, you'll normally have to consult an appraiser or gem laboratory, and even they may find it impossible to identify the type of filling present in some emeralds.

Tips on Selecting a $200, $2,000, and $20,000 Emerald Solitaire Ring

The higher the price of an emerald, the more you need to know about its clarity enhancement. Suppose you are buying a $200 half-carat emerald solitaire ring. All you need to know is that it has probably been fracture filled and that it therefore requires special care. Emeralds in jewelry of this price range are typically low quality, despite what ads may claim. The mountings are often worth more than the emeralds themselves.

Epoxies have become a preferred filling for low-priced emeralds because they last longer and hide the flaws better than oil. Thanks to epoxy fillers as well as oil, consumers can buy affordable emeralds that look acceptable.

If you're buying a $2,000 one-carat emerald solitaire ring, you should find out if colored fillers have been used on the emerald and if enhancement has had a major impact on its clarity. You wouldn't want to pay $1,800 or $1,900 for an emerald that in its unenhanced state is worth, say, $400. To avoid this, select an emerald with good transparency and as few surface cracks as possible. Deal with a salesperson who knows how to judge emerald quality and who will show you the stone under magnification. And have the stone examined by an independent appraiser. Guidelines for choosing a competent appraiser are given at the end of this chapter.

When buying a $20,000 emerald solitaire ring, it's in your interest to find out what type of filling is present as well as the degree of clarity enhancement. If you're spending nearly $20,000 on an emerald, you're probably not buying the stone just for its beauty and romance. Most likely you view your purchase partially as an investment. In this case, you should consider its marketability.

Many dealers would refuse to buy a $20,000 emerald treated with an epoxy, especially if the filler has been hardened. They don't want to spend that much money on a stone with a solidified filling that's difficult or impossible to take out. They also object to the goal of epoxy fillers--to hide cracks rather than de-emphasize them as oil does. Nobody wants to pay a large sum of money for an emerald with a lot of hidden cracks.

Colorless oil is an accepted emerald filler. Dealers will buy an expensive oiled emerald from you if it's worth the price asked and if the effect of the enhancement is minimal.

When buying a high-priced emerald, it's appropriate to ask the salesperson if they have any information on how it's been enhanced. If they tell you it's only been oiled and has not been filled with an epoxy, have them write this on the receipt.

Some stores provide lab reports with their stones. These are helpful aids; but for an expensive emerald, you should obtain your own documentation. Changes may have occurred in the emerald fillings since the store got the lab report, and the fillers might therefore be easier to identify. Also, the stone could have been treated after the report was issued.

For a $20,000 emerald, you should get two types of documents--an appraisal from an independent appraiser and a report from a major gem lab. Appraisals tell you what the stone is worth. Lab reports don't. Both documents should provide you with details about the identity of the stone. They may also include information on enhancements, country of origin, and/or quality.

Major laboratories have greater expertise, more sophisticated equipment and more opportunities to examine emeralds than the average jeweler or appraiser. As a result, they are better equipped to detect synthetics and enhancements, and their documents usually carry more weight when gems are bought and sold.

Some of the better known gem laboratories are listed alphabetically below along with the type of enhancement information they give on their emerald lab reports. A few of the labs will provide additional verbal information if you request it.

AGL (American Gemological Laboratories) 580 Fifth Ave. Suite 706, New York, NY 10036, phone (212) 704-0727
Indicate if clarity enhancement is faint, moderate, strong, or prominent and specify the type of filling when possible.

AIGS (Asian Institute of Gemological Sciences) Jewelry Trade Center, 919/1 Silom Road, Bangrak, Bangkok, 10500, phone (662) 267-4325/8 Fax (662) 267-4329
Notes if evidence of filled fissures is present and identifies the fillings as oil, colored oil, or resins or other similar colorless foreign substances.

EGL Los Angeles, (European Gemological Laboratory, Los Angeles) 550 S. Hill Suite 1595, Los Angeles, CA 90013, phone (213) 622-2387 or (800) 235-3287

Indicates if surface reaching fractures have been filled to enhance the stone's appearance and if the filling has been colored.

GAGTL (Gemmological Association and Gem Testing Laboratory of Great Britain) 27 Greville Street, London EC1N8SU, England, phone (O71) 404-3334 Fax (071) 404-8843

If a stone has been fracture filled, states "The emerald(s) described above show(s) evidence of filled fissures." Natural emeralds with a green or other-colored filling in fissures are described as "treated emeralds."

GIA (Gemological Institute of America) **Gem Trade Laboratory** 1630 Stewart St. Santa Monica, CA 90404, phone (310) 829-2991 or 580 Fifth Ave. New York, NY 10036-4794, phone (212) 221-5858

Notes if evidence of clarity or color enhancement is present.

Gübelin Gemmological Laboratory Maihofstrasse 102, CH 6000 Luzern 9, phone (041) 26 17 17, Fax (041) 26 17 34

Indicates there is evidence of clarity enhancement when it has a significant effect on the appearance. If the stone has not been filled, the report states no clarity enhancement is present.

SSEF Swiss Gemological Institute, Falknerstrasse 9, CH - 4001, Basel, Switzerland, phone (41 61) 262-0640 Fax (41 61) 262-0641

Writes under comments "No indication of fissure treatment" if an emerald shows no treatment. An emerald is called TREATED EMERALD when *colored* substances are found in the fissures.

Choosing a Competent Appraiser

There may be several people in your area who could do a high quality appraisal of a $50,000 diamond ring. There may only be one or two that could do one of a $5,000 emerald ring. Appraisers don't get as much experience valuing emeralds; emeralds are harder to identify than diamonds due to the proliferation of emerald synthetics and treatments; and there's no standardized system for grading colored stones as there is for diamonds. Consequently, finding a competent emerald appraiser can be a real challenge.

Three things you should consider when choosing an appraiser are their qualifications, their candor, and the thoroughness of their appraisals.

As for **qualifications**, an appraiser should have a gemologist diploma. The two best known diplomas are the **FGA** (Fellow of the Gemmological Association of Great

Britain) and the **GG** (Graduate Gemologist awarded by the Gemological Institute of America). Experience and education beyond the gemology courses are also essential. Titles issued in America that indicate advanced qualifications are:

AGA-CGL Accredited Gemologists Association Certified Gem Laboratory. Requirements include a written and practical exam, adequate equipment, and a background check of professional credentials.

CAPP Certified Appraiser of Personal Property, the highest award offered by the International Society of Appraisers. To receive it one must attend their appraisal courses and pass exams. Trade experience is a prerequisite.

CGA Certified Gemologist Appraiser, awarded by the American Gem Society to certified gemologists that pass their written and practical appraisal exam. Trade experience is a prerequisite.

MGA Master Gemologist Appraiser, the highest award offered by the American Society of Appraisers. To receive it, a person must pass their appraisal tests and have a gemologist diploma, an accredited gem lab, and at least 3 to 5 years appraisal experience.

Candor is as important a consideration as credentials. Ethical appraisers will not withhold relevant information from you to avoid offending a seller. They will talk openly about gem quality and treatments. They will also acknowledge their limitations. Appraising an emerald is not easy. If an appraiser tells you he/she doesn't feel qualified to appraise your emerald and recommends someone else, this is not a sign of incompetence. It's a sign of honesty. It's the same as a general medical doctor referring you to a specialist.

Competent appraisers provide **thorough appraisals**. A report that states, "18K ladies ring containing a 2-ct oval emerald with fine green color, value: $9,000" is not an adequate appraisal. If this ring were lost or stolen, an insurance policy would probably only cover the actual replacement value of the ring. Since there is no information about clarity, transparency, cut, or degree of enhancement, the insurance company could legally replace the ring with one containing a cheap heavily flawed, translucent emerald.

When choosing an appraiser, you should ask to see a sample of a colored stone appraisal. The report should include the following information:

♦ The identity of the stone(s) and metal(s)
♦ The measurements and estimated weights of the stones. (If you can tell appraisers the exact weight of the stones, this will help them give you a more accurate appraisal.

Therefore, when buying jewelry, ask stores to write on the receipt any stone weights listed on the sales tags.)

♦ A description of the color, clarity, transparency, shape, cutting style, and cut quality of the stones. The grading and color reference system used should also be indicated. Appraisers use different color communication systems to denote color. Three of the best known ones are GemDialogue, AGL Color/Scan, and GIA GemSet.

♦ A description of the mounting

♦ Relevant treatment information

Thorough appraisals might also include:

♦ A photograph of the piece and/or of the stone

♦ Plots of the inclusions in the stones (of either all or only the major stones)

♦ The country of origin of the stone(s) when this can be determined

♦ The name(s) of the manufacturers or designers of the piece when this is known

♦ A list of the tests performed and the instruments used

♦ Definitions or explanations of the terminology used on the report

Jewelry appraising is an art. There is a lot more to it than simply placing a dollar value on a stone or jewelry piece. If your jewelry has a great deal of monetary or sentimental value, it's important that you have a detailed, accurate appraisal of it. Take as much care in selecting your appraiser as you did with your jewelry.

10

Imitation or Real?

The inclusions in emerald and the unique mix of colors in tanzanite set these two gems apart from stones that imitate them. In the next section, you will learn how these and other clues can help you identify emerald and tanzanite.

Tests a Layperson Can Do

Three-Color Test

When you look at tanzanite from different angles, it will probably appear to be two different colors, violetish blue or purple (lavender in light colors). You may occasionally see a third color which may be green, yellow, red, orange, or brown or a mixture of any of these colors. This is because tanzanite is a combination of three colors seen in three different crystal directions. In technical terms, it is described as a **trichroic** (three-color) gem. Very few gems are trichroic and none display the same three colors as tanzanite. This makes it relatively easy to identify.

Fig. 10.1 Note the yellow, blue, and lavender colors on the pavilion of this tanzanite. It's unusual for all three trichroic colors to be visible simultaneously.

In light colors, tanzanite may be confused with iolite ("water sapphire"), another trichroic violetish-blue gem, which costs a lot less. Iolite is typically bluer than tanzanite, and, from the side view, it may appear near colorless rather than purple or blue.

In more intense colors, tanzanite may look like sapphire, which costs more. Sapphire, however, lacks the purplish highlights of tanzanite. And sapphire is a blend of just two colors--violetish blue and greenish blue. These two **dichroic** colors are easily visible through two polaroid filters placed side by side at right angles to each other. Color zoning and a heavy, asymmetric, bulged pavilion can also serve as visual clues that a stone is sapphire rather than tanzanite. Keep in mind, though, that sapphires are often evenly colored, and their cut proportions can resemble those of tanzanite.

Gemologists look for dichroic and trichroic colors in stones through a cylindrical instrument called a **dichroscope** (figure 10.2). One type is made with Polaroid material (about $45) and another with calcite (about $100). When you look at a well-lit stone through the correct end of a dichroscope, you'll see two squares. The squares can be two different colors if the stone is dichroic or trichroic. By rotating the dichroscope and looking at the stone **from several different angles**, you should be able to see the two or three colors the stone displays. In some directions only one color will be visible through the dichroscope. Occasionally, when viewing the pavilion through the dichroscope at a facet junction, it's possible to see all three trichroic colors at once. Normally, though, only one or two are visible at the same time.

Fig. 10.2 Dichroscope

As mentioned earlier, two polaroid filters or gels can be used to determine dichroism and trichroism. A dichroscope is usually easier to use, though. If you decide to buy one, have the salesperson show you how to use it with some sample stones.

Two-Color Test

This is a good test for emerald, which is a dichroic gem. Look at the unknown stone in different directions through a dichroscope or with perpendicular polaroid filters. If you can see a distinct bluish green and yellowish green side by side, then the stone is probably an emerald. Glass and green cubic zirconia, two common imitators of emerald, exhibit only one color.

This two-color test will not help you detect synthetic (lab-grown) emeralds. These have the same chemical composition and structure as the natural stone so they will show the same dichroism.

The Perfect Clarity Test

This is another good test for emerald. If the stone looks flawless under 10-power magnification, it's probably an imitation or a synthetic, especially if it's large and has a good depth of color (fig 10.4). Even good emeralds normally have inclusions, some of which are only found in natural emerald.

Fig. 10.3 Earrings set with glass stones in a closed back setting.

Fig. 10.4 Close-up view of a stone in Fig. 10.3. Note the tiny bubbles and near flawless appearance.

One common translucent imitation that tends to appear flawless is dyed green chalcedony. A couple of appraisers have told the author that it's often seen in antique jewelry and in pieces purchased from vendors in India. Occasionally, it is sold as emerald in stores in the United States.

Closed-Back Test

If the stone is set in jewelry, look at the back of the setting. Is the pavilion (bottom) of the stone blocked from view or enclosed in metal (fig. 10.3)? Normally, the bottom of a faceted emerald or tanzanite is at least partially visible. Therefore, if you can see only the crown (the top of the stone), you should be suspicious.

An open-back setting does not indicate a stone is genuine. Glass imitations are often set with the pavilion showing. But a completely closed back is often a sign that something is being hidden. Maybe the stone has a foil back or coating to add color and brilliance. Maybe the stone is made of two separate pieces of material that have been glued together. No matter what might be hidden, to avoid being duped, it is best to buy stones in a setting with part of the pavilion showing if you're not dealing with someone you know and trust.

The Price Test

Is the stone being sold at an unbelievably low price? If it is, it might be an imitation, synthetic, or stolen or defective merchandise. Even gem dealers rely on the price test to help them avoid being fooled by synthetics. They realize that a supplier can't stay in business if he sells stones below his cost.

The Glass Test

One of the most common imitations of emerald is glass. Some of the characteristics of glass are as follows:

♦ Gas bubbles (fig. 10.4). In glass they are round, oval, elongated, or shaped like donuts.
♦ Rounded facet edges (fig. 10.6). Real gems of good quality normally have sharper, more defined facet edges. Rounded girdles and facet edges can be found in low-quality emeralds.
♦ Concave facets and surfaces (fig. 10.6)
♦ Swirly lines or formations.
♦ Uneven or pitted surfaces. In some cases, the surface may resemble an orange peel.

The best way to learn to recognize glass, is to start looking at it closely. Look at some inexpensive drinking glasses with a loupe. There will probably be some bubbles and often they will be visible with the naked eye. Large bubbles are one of the most reliable indications of glass. Look at cheap costume jewelry with a loupe whenever you get a chance and try to find the characteristics above. The more you examine glass, the better you will become at identifying it.

Chelsea Filter Test

The Chelsea color filter was developed in the 1930's to help distinguish emeralds from green look-alikes such as glass, emerald triplets, and green sapphire (fig. 10.5). When you hold the filter to your eye and look through it at an emerald lit with an incandescent lamp, the emerald will typically look reddish or pinkish instead of green. Green sapphire and most green glass will look green.

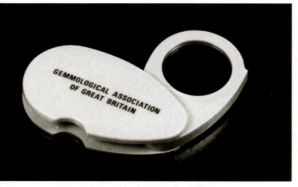

Fig. 10.5 Chelsea color filter

There are many instances when the Chelsea filter test does not work. Some African and Indian emeralds look green through the filter. Many emerald look-alikes appear reddish or pinkish; for example, green zircon, demantoid garnet, dyed green chalcedony, tsavorite, green fluorite, chrome tourmaline, chrome diopside, green YAG, green synthetic sapphire, many synthetic emeralds, some hiddenite, some glass, some plastic, some green synthetic spinel. The chelsea filter may also not work if fluorescent lighting is used. For best results, use an incandescent lamp.

The chelsea filter is more helpful for detecting the presence of chromium in emeralds than for spotting fakes. Emeralds with a high chromium content will generally look pink or red through the filter. This is useful information when you want to know if an emerald may be Colombian. Colombian emeralds are typically colored by chromium so they will usually show a pinkish or reddish reaction.

Fig. 10.6 Concave facets and a rounded girdle and facet edges are evidence that this is a glass stone.

Fig. 10.7 The ring which contains the glass stone seen in figure 10.6

Fig. 10.8 This ring contains natural emeralds and diamonds, but it is not valuable. These poorly cut, highly flawed, translucent emeralds might wholesale for $5-$15 a carat. An illusion type setting makes the industrial-quality diamonds look larger than they actually are.

When a stone has an unusually strong red appearance through the chelsea filter, you should suspect it might be synthetic. Occasionally, Columbian emeralds show a similar strong reaction, but this is not common.

The chelsea filter has a variety of other uses. For example, some dyed jadeite will look pinkish through the filter. Non-dyed green jadeite looks green. Therefore a pinkish reaction to the chelsea filter test indicates the presence of dye in green jadeite. Chelsea filters cost about $40 and are available through jewelry supply stores, the GIA, and the British Gemmological Association.

Other Ways of Identifying Emeralds and Tanzanite

Many of the other identification tests require special training and equipment. Nevertheless, you may be curious about how gemologists identify emeralds and tanzanite. Three of the most important methods are given below:

♦ The **refractive index** (the degree to which light is bent as it passes through the stone) is determined. This is measured with an instrument called a refractometer. Natural emeralds have a refractive index of 1.577-1.583 (±.017), which means they bend light about 1.58 times more than air does. This also means that light travels 1.58 times more slowly through emerald than it does through air. (The emerald R.I. data is from the *GIA Gem Reference Guide*.)

There is no other dichroic emerald imitation that has the same refractive index (**R.I.**). Most lab-grown emeralds have a slightly lower R.I. than their natural counterpart. Consequently, the refractometer can be a useful tool for identifying both natural and synthetic emerald.

Note that the R.I. of natural emeralds may vary by a factor of ± .017. There is often a correlation between place of origin and R.I. due to the different impurities found in emeralds from the various localities. (A comparative R.I. list of emeralds from about 30 areas is provided by I.A Mumme on pages 91-92 of his book *The Emerald*.) The presence of oil or other emerald fillers may also have a slight effect on the R.I. reading.

The refractive index of tanzanite is 1.691-1.700, a lot higher than the R.I. of iolite (1.542-1.551) and lower than that of sapphire (1.762-1.770).

♦ The interior and exterior of the stone are examined under high magnification. Certain features such as those listed in the chapter on clarity are characteristic of emerald and tanzanite. The microscope is the most helpful tool for identifying natural emeralds.

♦ A light is directed through the stone with an instrument called a spectroscope to measure how it absorbs light. Emerald and tanzanite have characteristic readings.

Distinguishing emerald and tanzanite from other gem species and glass is not hard if a combination of the preceding tests are done correctly. What can be hard, however, is to separate natural from synthetic emerald. That topic will be addressed in the next chapter.

Deceptive Practices

A stone can be a natural emerald and still in a sense be a fake. Many techniques have been devised to trick buyers into thinking a stone is better quality than it actually is. Listed below are practices that are normally done with the intent to deceive. All of them, however, can be considered legitimate when they are properly disclosed to buyers.

Coatings

Varnish, plastic, paint and dyed fingernail polish are among the substances used to coat emeralds. Normally this is done to make the stone appear greener and therefore more valuable.

Sometimes only the bottom of the emerald is coated. If the stone is set in a closed back mounting the coating may be difficult to spot. Magnification is usually the best way to detect coatings. Bubbles, spotty color, peeled facet edges, or uneven, unpolished surfaces are signs of coating. To avoid buying a coated emerald, select jewelry with open-back settings, deal with a reputable jeweler, and decline deals that sound too good to be true.

Fig. 10.9 Bottom of a glass stone that has lost most of its foil backing.

Fig. 10.10 Sometimes foil backings are visible on stones set in closed back mountings.

Foil Backing

Foil backings have been used to add color and brilliance to gems for probably 4000 years (figs. 10.9 & 10.10). As gem-cutting techniques progressed and brought out more brilliance in stones, these backings became less popular. Today foil backings are occasionally found on pale emeralds, but they are more likely to be seen on glass imitations. Antique jewelry buyers should be especially alert to the possibility of foil backings since they used to be very common. Beware of closed-back settings. Foil may be concealed, particularly if a stone is unusually bright.

Quench Crackling

Stones that are quench crackled have been heated and then plunged into cold water. This procedure is done to produce cracks in some lab-grown emeralds so they'll look more natural.

In India, fake emeralds were often made by quench crackling rock crystal (colorless quartz) and then filling it with green oil or dye. Low-grade aquamarine, emerald or colorless beryl may also be processed in this manner to create emerald fakes.

Composite Stones (Assembled Stones)

Composite stones are formed by cementing together two or more pieces of a gem material or glass. When stones are composed of two parts, they are called **doublets**. Stones consisting of three parts are **triplets**. Two-piece stones fused with a colored transparent cement are also referred to as triplets. The colored cement is considered a third component, making it a triplet.

Tanzanite doublets are made by gluing tanzanite crowns to glass (*Gemstones of the World* by Walter Schumann, pg. 160).

Emerald triplets consist of two pieces of pale emerald that are joined together with a green gelatin or cement layer. In addition, green composite stones made not of emerald but of colorless beryl, pale aquamarine, quartz, or colorless synthetic spinel are incorrectly called "emerald" triplets. In Europe, these type of green assembled stones are called **"emerald" doublets** or **soudé "emeralds"** (French for soldered "emerald".

Some emerald triplets are sold with proper disclosure. Needless to say, you should not pay a lot of money for them.

The key to identifying a composite stone is to find where its parts have been joined (fig. 10.11). In loose stones, this may be easy to see. In mounted stones, it's usually difficult to detect. However, when you look at the stones face-up under magnification, you can sometimes see flattened air bubbles between the parts, glue around the edge of the stone, or swirly areas where the stone has been brushed with the bonding agent (fig. 10.12). These are indications of a composite stone.

Loose stones can be checked by immersing them in water. In water, the stones will look near colorless from the side except for the green cement layer. Alcohol and methylene iodide are also used as immersion liquids. However, stones suspected of being emerald or of having a colored glue should not be put in these two liquids. They could either dissolve the oil used to fill emeralds or attack the colored cement.

Fig. 10.11 Side view of a colorless-beryl triplet. A dark green line is visible around the girdle where the two parts of the stone have been joined with a colored cement. When this stone is immersed in water, the pavilion and crown appear colorless from the side view.

Fig. 10.12 Face-up view of same triplet. Bubbles and glue around the edge are clearly visible. These clues are not always this obvious.

Misnomers

Sometimes stones are sold under misleading names to make them seem more valuable. If a salesperson adds a qualifying word to a gem name, always ask him to explain what it means. Some emerald misnomers are as follows:

African emerald	sometimes a misnomer for green fluorite
Brazilian emerald	sometimes a misnomer for green tourmaline
Emerald triplet/doublet	often a misnomer for a triplet or doublet made from quartz, synthetic spinel or colorless beryl

Evening emerald	peridot
Indian emerald	dyed crackled quartz
Kongo emerald	dioptase
Lithia emerald	hiddenite
Medina emerald	green glass
Mt. St. Helen's emerald	green glass, which is also referred to as *Emerald Obsidianite*. It contains at most 5% to 10% of Mount Saint Helen's ash, if any, according to an article by Kurt Nassau in the Summer 1986 issue of *Gems & Gemology* (pp 103-104).
Night emerald	peridot
Oriental emerald	green sapphire
Pseudo emerald	malachite
Spanish emerald	green glass
Soudé emerald	a green composite stone
Tecla emerald	a green composite stone

Avoiding Gem Scams

During the past decade, gem scams have proliferated. Some consumers have lost their life savings and their homes because of gem "investment" schemes. To avoid being duped by scam artists, follow the guidelines below.

♦ **Do not buy expensive jewelry and gems through the mail or over the phone if you don't know the seller.** A high percentage of gem scam victims have bought their stones from telemarketers and mail-order operators. You have to examine a stone both with and without magnification to know if it's worth buying.

♦ **Avoid gem investment schemes even when the stones come with lab reports.** Legitimate dealers do not promise high annual returns on gem investments. No one can guarantee that the value of a gem will go up or that it will be easy to resell. Scam artists love to impress their victims with lab reports that are either phoney or that lack pertinent quality details.

♦ **Do not buy gems in sealed plastic containers which you are not allowed to open.** Clear plastic covers can mask gem flaws and cutting defects. People involved in gem scams often sell sealed stones with a written warning such as "Breaking the seal will invalidate all guarantees." The purpose of the tamper-proof containers is to prevent independent examination. Legitimate dealers will allow you to look at the stone outside of its packet or container.

♦ **Keep in mind that lab reports are not appraisals**. Internationally respected labs do not indicate the monetary value of stones on their reports. They provide technical information about gemstone identity, enhancement, country of origin, and/or quality. The GIA, for example, has high-tech equipment which can detect synthetics, so their reports are very helpful for confirming if an emerald is natural. However, GIA reports do not provide any information about the quality or value of colored stones. Therefore you should not assume a stone is valuable just because it comes with a GIA report stating it is a natural emerald. Natural emeralds come in all price ranges. To find out what a stone is worth, you need to get an appraisal.

♦ **Get your own appraisals and lab reports.** Don't rely on those provided by the seller. If you were buying a classic car, you wouldn't go to the seller's mechanic to have the car checked. You'd take it to your own. Likewise, when you're buying gems, you should take them to an appraiser who has your interests in mind, not the seller's. Appraisals paid for by the seller are not independent appraisals.

♦ **Don't be greedy.** People who expect abnormally high returns on their money are the most likely to become victims of scams. Even with legitimate investments, the higher the potential gain the greater the risk of loss.

♦ **Keep in mind that lab reports are not appraisals**. Internationally respected labs do not indicate the monetary value of stones on their reports. They provide technical information about gemstone identity, enhancement, country of origin, and/or quality. The GIA, for example, has high-tech equipment which can detect synthetics, so their reports are very helpful for confirming if an emerald is natural. However, GIA reports do not provide any information about the quality or value of colored stones. Therefore you should not assume a stone is valuable just because it comes with a GIA report stating it is a natural emerald. Natural emeralds come in all price ranges. To find out what a stone is worth, you need to get an appraisal.

♦ **Get your own appraisals and lab reports.** Don't rely on those provided by the seller. If you were buying a classic car, you wouldn't go to the seller's mechanic to have the car checked. You'd take it to your own. Likewise, when you're buying gems, you should take them to an appraiser who has your interests in mind, not the seller's. Appraisals paid for by the seller are not independent appraisals.

♦ **Don't be greedy.** People who expect abnormally high returns on their money are the most likely to become victims of scams. Even with legitimate investments, the higher the potential gain the greater the risk of loss.

11

Synthetic Emeralds

If you've ever shopped for vitamin C, you've probably noticed two basic types--natural and non-natural. The natural Vitamin C comes from natural sources and costs more. The non-natural type was synthesized in a laboratory with chemicals.

Similarly, natural emerald is mined in nature and synthetic emerald is grown in a lab. Both synthetic vitamin C and synthetic emerald have essentially the same chemical composition as their natural counterparts. Neither one is an imitation.

According to *Webster's New Collegiate Dictionary* (7th edition), a synthetic is "a product of chemical synthesis." To the average person on the street, though, a synthetic is a fake. As a result, the marketers of synthetic emeralds prefer to use terms such as **lab-grown**, **created**, **cultured**, or **man-made** to describe their product. Gemologists and natural stone dealers usually identify created emeralds as synthetic.

Most trade members use the term **natural emerald** to mean an emerald formed in the earth. They don't use it to also mean "untreated emerald". This trade usage of "natural" applies to all gems. For example, a dyed pearl formed by an oyster without the aid of man is called a natural pearl of non-natural color or simply a dyed natural pearl. Since "natural" can have a dual meaning, some gemologists label mined emeralds as "emeralds of natural origin"

The jewelry industry is not alone in their usage of "natural". Natural Vitamin C is processed, and it's not exactly the same as the vitamin C in orange juice. The label "natural" merely means the vitamin is of natural origin and not made from chemicals in a laboratory.

Synthetic Versus Natural

Synthetic emeralds have the same crystal structure and chemical formula ($Be_3Al_2(SiO_3)_6$) as natural emerald as well as similar physical and optical properties. However, they differ in the following ways:

Price. Lab-grown emeralds cost a lot less than natural emeralds of similar appearance. In 1994, high-quality created emeralds were retailing for about $150 a carat at some public gem shows. Their price did vary somewhat according to quality and size. Some manufactures charge more for larger stones. Others charge more for small sizes to pay for cutting costs.

Do not assume that an emerald is worth a lot just because it's natural. A lot of low-grade natural emerald sells for less than synthetic emerald. You must always consider the quality of the stone.

Appearance. One of the biggest advantages of lab-grown emeralds is that they look attractive and expensive, yet they are a lot more affordable than high-quality natural emeralds.

Rarity. Lab-grown emeralds can be produced in whatever quantities are needed. As a result, they are readily available. High quality natural emeralds are very rare and therefore are extremely valuable. Finding a good-quality natural emerald in the size or shape you'd like can be difficult. You may have to compromise on size, quality, or color.

Absence of fillers. Unlike natural emerald, synthetics are normally not fracture-filled. Low-grade synthetic material, however, is occasionally filled with either colorless or colored substances.

Growing Time. Lab-grown emeralds usually take less than a year to grow. Natural emeralds are formed over a period of millions of years. Since natural emeralds cannot be produced quickly by nature, their supply is limited, which in turn means they are more highly valued.

Durability. Lab-grown emeralds generally have fewer inclusions and fractures than natural emeralds. As a result they are more durable.

Synthetic emeralds grown by the flux process are a lot more resistant to high heat than natural emerald (the flux process is described in the next section). Water which is present within the structure of natural emerald will expand if an emerald is heated. This can create stress on the emerald and cause it to break. Flux-grown emeralds, which contain no water, can be slowly heated to red heat and remain unaffected. Kurt Nassau points out this fact in his book *Gems Made by Man*, page 128. Naturally, you should not do this test yourself.

Thanks to their greater durability and lack of fillers, many synthetic emeralds can be cleaned in ultrasonic cleaners. Four brand-names of lab-grown emerald that can withstand ultrasonic cleaning are Empress, Inamori, Kimberley, and Regency. No lab-grown emerald with fractures, however, should undergo ultrasonic cleaning. The motion of the mechanism can enlarge the fractures, and the cleaning solution could partially dissolve any filling material that might be present.

Potential for Price Appreciation. The price of high-quality natural emeralds has increased over the years whereas the price of created emeralds has gone down significantly. In 1994, one manufacturer dropped its prices by as much as 45%. Previously, one of the main criticisms some jewelers had of synthetic emeralds was their high cost. The better qualities could retail for over $700 per carat. Thanks to increased competition, synthetic emeralds are now a lot more affordable.

Types of Synthetic Emerald

Not all synthetic emeralds look alike. This is because they are made by different manufacturers and processes. There are two basic kinds of synthetic emerald: flux and hydrothermal.

The **flux** type is made by dissolving nutrients (the chemicals needed to make emerald) in a molten chemical called a flux. Then for a period up to about a year, the nutrients gradually crystallize. Emerald crystals were first produced with this process in 1848 by Jacques Ebelman, a French chemist. In the 1930's, Carroll Chatham became the first to develop this emerald growing process into a commercially viable one. His company is still the largest producer of flux-growth emeralds. These stones are marketed as **Chatham** created emeralds. Some other brands or manufacturers of flux-growth emeralds are **Crystural**, **Empress**, **Gilson**, **Inamori** by Kyocera, **Lennix**, and **Seiko**.

Hydrothermal synthetic emeralds are made by dissolving nutrients at high temperatures and pressures in a solution of water and chemicals. One part of the container is kept cool enough to allow crystallization. This process is more like natural gem formation than the flux method. During the past few years, the demand for hydrothermal emeralds has increased significantly because they usually cost less than the flux type. Two brands of hydrothermal emerald that are currently being sold are **Regency** and **Kimberley** (also called "Biron"). There is also a lot of generic Russian hydrothermal emerald on the market.

Synthetic emerald coatings have been grown on faceted aquamarine and colorless beryl. This material is not true synthetic emerald but rather "synthetic-emerald coated beryl" or "beryl with a synthetic emerald overgrowth."

117

Tests to Detect Synthetic Emeralds

Since synthetic emeralds grow in a laboratory rather than in nature, they have distinguishing characteristics. Hydrothermal emeralds are usually the most difficult to detect because their growing process most closely resembles that of natural emeralds. Listed below are some tests for separating synthetic from natural emeralds. Laypeople can do the first four tests. The last five tests require more expensive equipment and technical expertise. You may wish to skip over them and go to the next section, which offers practical buying tips.

Color Test

Compare the color of the stone to that of other emeralds you've seen. Does it look natural? If not, the stone may be synthetic, especially if the price is unusually low and the color is highly saturated.

Synthetic Emerald Filter Test

A color filter that separates most synthetic emerald from natural emerald was discovered in 1993 by Alan Hodgkinson, a Scottish gemologist. If an emerald is synthetic, its body color will usually turn pinkish or reddish when viewed through the filter under an incandescent lamp or sunlight. If the emerald is natural, it will look greenish or lose body color. Two exceptions are Russian hydrothermal emerald and Kimberley (Biron) created emerald. These two synthetics respond as natural emeralds.

This color filter, also known as the Hanneman-Hodgkinson synthetic emerald filter, is intended to be a screening tool, not a definitive test. It costs $24 U.S. or £17 plus shipping and is available by writing to Hanneman Gemological Instruments, PO Box 734, Poulsbo, WA 98370 or to Alan Hodgkinson, Whinhurst, Portencross by Westkilbride, Ayrshire, Scotland KA 23 9PZ. The synthetic emerald filter is easy for laypeople to use, but they should first read the instructions and try out the filter with known synthetic and natural emeralds.

Chelsea Filter Test

Hold the filter to your eye and look at the stone through it under an incandescent lamp (see Chelsea filter test in Chapter 10). Most synthetic emeralds will have a stronger red appearance than natural emeralds. There are a few exceptions. Russian hydrothermal emeralds look green through the filter. Some fine Colombian emeralds, on the other hand, show a strong red reaction.

Inclusion Test

Look at the stone with and without magnification to determine if it has any flaws. If none are visible, the stone is probably synthetic.

Hydrothermal synthetic emeralds are noted for their high clarity and transparency. When inclusions are present, they tend to resemble those of natural emeralds. One distinguishing characteristic of hydrothermal emeralds is their unusual growth patterns (fig. 11.1). These are often visible through a 10-power hand magnifier, but they are easier to identify using a microscope. To find these growth features, you normally have to view the stones from different angles. You may also need to use different types of lighting. The growth patterns in figure 11.1 were visible both with transmitted and overhead lighting.

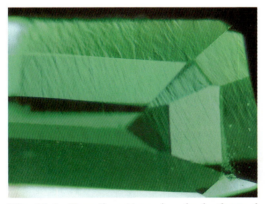

Fig. 11.1 Growth patterns in a hydrothermal synthetic emerald. As you tilt the stone, they seem to disappear.

Fig. 11.2 Flux inclusions in a Chatham created emerald. *Photo courtesy GIA.*

Flux inclusions resembling fingerprints and veils are common in flux-grown emerald. Their high relief, opaqueness, and often granular texture help us distinguish them from similar inclusions in natural emerald (fig 11.2). If the inclusions remain whitish and non-transparent as the stone is tilted back and forth, they are likely to be flux inclusions.

Sindi Schloss, an appraiser and instructor in Arizona, has helped her students detect synthetics by giving them the following guideline: "As a general rule, natural emeralds have **combinations** of inclusion types (different colored crystals, liquid inclusions, needles, etc.), whereas synthetics tend to be more homogeneous (i.e. flux have flux fingerprints, hydrothermal have chevron growth patterns, etc.)".

Identifying inclusions requires a lot of skill and practice. That's why it's important for you to look at emeralds under magnification whenever possible. You will gradually learn to recognize some of the inclusions typically found in natural and synthetic emeralds. Keep in mind that you may need to use high magnification and a variety of lighting techniques to locate some emerald inclusions.

The appendix of this book lists characteristic inclusions of emeralds from various localities and manufacturers. Two sources that provide a lot of photo examples of emerald inclusions are *Photoatlas of Inclusions in Gemstones* by Eduard Gübelin & John Koivula and *Esmeraldas, Inclusões em Gemes* by Dietmar Schwarz. If you can read Spanish, you'll probably be able to decipher the Portuguese photo captions.

Crossed-Polaroid Test

A microscope and two polaroid filters are required for this test. One filter threads onto the microscope below the optic objectives and the other fits into the light well. The filters are rotated to a crossed, dark position. If stones are examined under this cross-polarized light, they may provide evidence of synthetic origin. Kimberley and Russian hydrothermal emeralds can show distinctive patterns of illumination (fig. 11.3). These patterns are not seen in natural and flux-synthetic emeralds (fig 11.4).

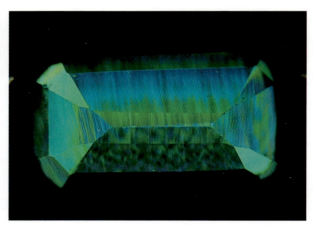

Fig. 11.3 Colorful patterns of a hydrothermal emerald viewed under magnification between crossed polaroid filters.

Fig. 11.4 Left: Note the absence of the patterns in two natural emeralds and a small oval flux emerald. These stones were photographed in the same way as the one in figure 11.3.

Gemologist Alan Hodgkinson has observed that between crossed polaroid filters, Kimberley (Biron) hydrothermal emeralds show "jagged peak inclusions resembling swallows in flight" (figs. 11.5 & 11.6). He adds that Russian hydrothermal emeralds "appear as a pattern reminiscent of a well-known ornamental plate-glass door panel" (figs. 11.5 & 11.7). To locate these patterns, you must hold the stone in various positions because the patterns are only visible when viewed at specific angles.

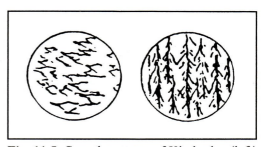

Fig. 11.5 Growth patterns of Kimberley (left) and Russian hydrothermal emeralds (right). *Diagram courtesy Alan Hodgkinson.*

Fig. 11.6 Growth patterns peculiar to Biron (Kimberley) hydrothermal emeralds. *Photo courtesy Alan Hodgkinson..*

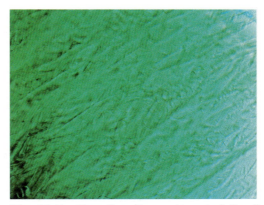

Fig. 11.7 Growth patterns characteristic of Russian hydrothermal emeralds. *Photo courtesy Alan Hodgkinson.*

Specific Gravity Test

This test measures the relative density of stones by comparing their weight to the weight of an equal volume of water. In other words, the **specific gravity (S.G.)** of a gemstone is the ratio of its density to the density of water.

The specific gravity of natural emerald is relatively low compared to other gemstones--2.72 (+.18, -.05) (GIA Gem Reference Guide). It can vary according to place of origin due to slight differences in chemical composition. A table listing the specific gravities of emeralds from various regions can be found in *The Emerald* by I. A. Mumme, pages 89-90.

The specific gravity of flux synthetic emeralds is normally lower than that of natural emerald. Chatham created emeralds, whose S.G. is 2.66, will generally float in a heavy liquid with an S.G. of 2.67 whereas natural emeralds will sink (however, some heavily flawed natural emeralds may float). The S.G. values of hydrothermal emeralds overlap the S.G. range of natural emeralds, so they cannot be separated with specific gravity tests. (Emeralds with surface breaks should not be placed in heavy liquids. These liquids might partially dissolve fracture fillings or remain in the emerald.)

Refractive Index Test

Synthetic emeralds usually have a slightly lower refractive index (R.I.) than natural emeralds. For example, Chatham lab-grown emeralds normally have a low R.I. reading of 1.561 and a high one of 1.564. The numerical difference between these two readings is .003 and is called its **birefringence**. Natural emeralds have an R.I. of 1.577-1.583 (±.017) and their birefringence is .005 to .009 (data from the *GIA Gem Reference Guide*). Therefore refractive index and birefringence can help distinguish natural from synthetic emeralds.

The refractive indices of synthetic emeralds can vary depending on their brand-name and method of growth. Hydrothermally-grown emeralds tend to have slightly higher R.I. and birefringence readings than the flux-growth type. These readings are listed in the appendix.

Fluorescence Test

Synthetic emeralds tend to show a distinctive fluorescence when viewed under long-wave ultraviolet light. Two exceptions are the Biron/Kimberley and Russian hydrothermal emeralds, which do not fluoresce. Most natural emeralds are inert to ultraviolet light although some chromium-rich emeralds fluoresce orangy red to red. The oil in natural emeralds may show a yellowish green to greenish yellow fluorescence under long-wave radiation. A list of the fluorescent reactions of various synthetics is given in the appendix.

Infrared Spectra Test

Gem laboratories find this test especially useful for identifying stones that have no distinguishing inclusions. This test can quickly detect the presence of water in emeralds. If no water is present, the stone is a flux synthetic. Natural and hydrothermal emeralds always contain water due to their growth conditions whereas water is absent in the structure of flux emeralds. More information on infrared spectra tests is available in an article by Carol Stockton in the summer 1987 issue of *Gems & Gemology*, pages 96-99.

Tips on Buying Synthetic Emeralds

Green CZ (cubic zirconia) *is made in a lab so it's okay to call it lab-grown emerald.*

This is what one salesperson told the author. It's true that CZ is a lab-grown stone, but it is not lab-grown emerald. It is lab-grown CZ. The retail price difference between the two stones is about $150 or more per carat.

Some stores call lab-grown emeralds "created emeralds" and they use the term "synthetic emerald" to refer to green glass or CZ. They misrepresent their imitation stones because "synthetic emerald" sounds better than "green glass". The terms "synthetic," "lab-grown," and "created" all have the same meaning.

Sometimes, the term **cultured** is used to mean "lab-grown" even though the two terms are not equivalent. In addition, consumers are often told that lab-grown emeralds are like cultured pearls. Culturing pearls is a more natural process than growing emeralds. A cultured pearl has a nacre coating that is grown in a natural organism and secreted by a natural organism. Man just inserts the irritant into the mollusk. On the other hand, a "cultured" emerald is grown in a lab, not in a natural environment such as the ground; and the chemical ingredients are supplied by man, not by nature through a natural process. It's unfair to the pearl industry and confusing to the public when crystal growers falsely equate growing emeralds to culturing pearls. This has led many salespeople and consumers to believe cultured pearls are grown in a laboratory when in fact they grow in oysters or mussels in lakes, bays, gulfs, etc.

Since terminology is so often misused, you'll need to clarify with salespeople what they mean by terms such as "synthetic," "lab-grown" or "created." To make sure that an emerald is in fact synthetic and not imitation, ask the salespeople what the difference is between a synthetic emerald and a fake one. If they can't tell you synthetic emerald is man-made emerald that has essentially the same chemical composition and structure as natural emerald, then they might sell you a fake as a synthetic emerald. This is basic information which salespeople should be familiar with because it is easily found in major trade magazines, books, and gemology courses.

Also ask the salespeople if the emerald has a brand name. If it has one of the names listed in this chapter, then it's likely to be a true synthetic emerald. If they tell you it's a flux or hydrothermal emerald, that's also a good indication it's not fake.

Buying a synthetic emerald can be almost as challenging as buying a natural one. The following guidelines will help you make a wise choice:

Pay attention to quality differences. Lab-grown emeralds come in a range of qualities, and sometimes there isn't much of a price difference between clean well-cut stones and lower quality ones. Evaluate lab-growns in the same way you would a natural stone. If you find a jewelry piece you like but the synthetic emerald in it is not good quality, ask if the stone can be changed. Some stores will do this at no extra charge.

Examine the stone under magnification just as you would a natural emerald. This will help you compare stones and spot fractures that may affect durability.

Ask the salesperson if the stone(s) can be cleaned ultrasonically. One of the major advantages of many synthetic emeralds is that they can be safely cleaned ultrasonically. Take advantage of this benefit by selecting stones that can be cleaned in this manner.

Make sure the receipt states the stone's identity and any other pertinent information. You'll then have a legal right to return the stone or jewelry piece if the synthetic emeralds turn out to be fake. Written details are also helpful for appraisal and insurance purposes.

Deal with knowledgeable, candid salespeople. They'll give you a lot of accurate information that will help you make a wise choice.

12

Caring for Your
Emerald & Tanzanite Jewelry

Sandy wanted to buy an emerald ring with her graduation money. She figured her aunt who was a gemologist could find her one for less than $200. Her aunt suggested getting a ring with a more affordable and durable stone, but Sandy wanted one with natural emerald(s) because that was her birthstone. She didn't mind if it would require special care and if the stones were of mediocre quality. Eventually her aunt found her a ring for $185. It had three small deep green emeralds and two tiny diamonds, and Sandy was very pleased with it.

Three years later, her aunt had a look at the ring. The emeralds were still green, but several "new" inclusions and colorless areas were easy to see under magnification even though the ring had never been cleaned ultrasonically. One stone was badly chipped on two different sides. Because Sandy has received many compliments on the ring and still really likes it, she is considering replacing the natural emeralds with synthetic ones. Since the natural emeralds have sentimental value, she will have two of them re-oiled and set in stud earrings.

Sandy does not regret her purchase. She has gotten more than $200 worth of pleasure and compliments from her ring. However, she has decided that in the future, she will reserve her natural emeralds for pendants, earrings, and pins. That way the stones will avoid the wear and exposure to dirt that her rings are subjected to.

This true story illustrates some of the problems that can occur with emeralds--chipping, change of clarity, and color lightening. The less the emeralds are worth and the more wear the stones are subjected to, the more likely it is that these problems will arise. Tanzanite is also a fragile stone, but since it is not treated with oil, epoxy, or colored substances, it does not change clarity or color.

Even though emeralds are not as hard as diamonds, rubies and sapphires, they are harder than most other gems (7.5 to 8 on the Mohs hardness scale of 1 to 10). Tanzanites are a little softer (6 to 7) so they can be scratched and abraded more easily than emeralds. Abraded tanzanites can be repolished to look like new, but it's best to avoid abrasions in the first place by treating the stones with special care.

Cleavage is the tendency for a mineral to split along crystal planes. It's the presence of fractures in emeralds and the perfect cleavage of tanzanite which make them vulnerable to knocks and to the vibrations of ultrasonic cleaners. Emeralds with no cracks can be cleaned ultrasonically. George Bosshart, director of the Gübelin Gemmological Laboratory, points this out in the October 1991 issue of the *Journal of Gemmology* (p 501). He writes:

> Emeralds are not necessarily endangered by ultrasonics. Beryls are not more brittle or friable than many other gemstones. They even lack a proper cleavage. The reaction of emeralds to any mechanical stress is dependent--as in the case of oil treatment--primarily on their quality. Every kind of gemstone with definite tension and cleavage cracks presents a higher risk than a stone without flaws. But even these can be damaged in extreme circumstances. For instance when a sharp girdle of a diamond baguette exerts pressure on a set emerald.

Jewelry professionals generally advise that emeralds never be placed in ultrasonics. This is because most emeralds have cracks and these cracks have oil or epoxy fillings which mask fractures and which may be dissolved over a period of time by cleaning solutions. Synthetic emeralds generally have a better clarity than their natural counterparts, and good-quality stones contain no fillings. Therefore, several of the synthetic emerald manufacturers state their stones can be safely cleaned in ultrasonics.

Cleaning and Care Tips

Risky cleaning procedures can often be avoided if you clean your jewelry on a regular basis. Tanzanites can be soaked in lukewarm soapy water using a mild liquid detergent. It's best not to soak emeralds because soap that is designed to cut grease can also gradually dissolve oil fillers. Simply rub the emeralds with a soapy cloth, rinse with cool water and dry with a lint-free cloth. Or, you may wish to spray the stones with a window cleaner and then wipe them off with the cloth. If the dirt on the stones cannot be removed with the cloth, try using a toothpick or unwaxed dental floss. If dirt still remains, then have the stones professionally cleaned by your jeweler. Never soak emeralds in alcohol, acetone or paint thinner. These are solvents which can rapidly dissolve oil fillings.

Jewelry care involves more than just proper cleaning. Further guidelines are as follows:

♦ Avoid exposing your jewelry to sudden changes of temperature. If you wear it in a hot tub and then go in cold water with it on or go from a hot oven to cold sink water, the stones could crack or shatter. Also keep jewelry away from steam and hot pots and ovens in the kitchen.

♦ Avoid wearing jewelry (especially rings) while participating in contact sports or doing housework, gardening, repairs, etc. In fact, it's a good idea to take your emerald and tanzanite jewelry off when you come home and change into casual clothes. Emeralds and tanzanites can become chipped, scratched, cracked and abraded more easily than stones like diamonds. Treat these gems as you would fine silk garments. With proper care, emerald and tanzanite pieces can last a lifetime.

♦ Store jewelry separately in soft material, pouches, or in padded jewelry bags with individual pockets. If a piece is placed next to or on top of other jewelry, the metal mountings or the stones can get scratched.

♦ Keep your emeralds away from hot lights, the sun, and any other source of heat because they can make the filler evaporate more quickly. The filler can also discolor or whitish particles can form. This means it's not advisable to wear emerald jewelry to the beach or leave it sitting on a window sill. Tanzanites are not normally affected by sunlight. However, they should be kept away from hot areas to avoid thermal shock like kitchen heat and hot water.

♦ Occasionally check your jewelry for loose stones. Shake it or tap it lightly with your forefinger while holding it next to your ear. If you hear the stones rattle or click, have a jeweler tighten the prongs.

♦ When you set jewelry near a sink, make sure the drains are plugged or that it's put in a protective container or on a spindle. Otherwise, don't take the jewelry off.

♦ Take a photo of your jewelry (a macro lens is helpful). Just lay it all together on a table for the photo. If the jewelry is ever lost or stolen, you'll have documentation to help you remember and prove what you had.

♦ About every six months, have a jewelry professional check your ring for loose stones or wear on the mounting. Many jewelers will do this free of charge, and they'll be happy to answer your questions regarding the care of your jewelry.

Options for People Who Want an Emerald Engagement Ring

People whose birthstone is emerald or whose favorite color is green sometimes want emerald engagement rings. Most emeralds will not withstand a lifetime of daily wear in a ring, nor can they undergo the ultrasonic cleanings required to maintain their brilliance and sparkle. Listed below are some ways to avoid these problems.

♦ Consider buying an emerald wedding or engagement pendant. Pendants are not subjected to the wear and dirt and lotions that rings are. Pendants and lockets have traditionally been given as symbols of love and commitment. The necklace has the same eternal circular form as the ring.

♦ Select a loose, lighter-colored emerald with a high clarity and no fractures. The lighter an emerald is, the less likely it is to have cracks and the easier it is to see cracks. Emeralds without fractures are less susceptible to chipping, can be cleaned ultrasonically and have no fillings which can deteriorate. Lighter colored emeralds are also more affordable. Since mountings can hide flaws, it's best to select a loose emerald and have it set in a ring mounting. Be sure the salesperson has a good knowledge of emeralds and can help you locate fractures. You will need assistance.

♦ If you want a deep-green emerald for a ring, select a small one with a high clarity and no fractures. The larger an emerald is, the more likely it is to have cracks. A top-quality 1-carat emerald would be considered by some as too rare and valuable to be subjected to the wear of an everyday ring.

♦ If you just want a gem that's green, you may wish to choose a stone such as jade or tsavorite (a green garnet). Both are suitable for rings, but jade is more durable. In fact, due to its internal structure, jade is more durable than any other colored gem. Imperial jade comes the closest to having an emerald green color, but be sure its color is natural and not dyed. Tsavorite tends to be a little more yellowish-green. It does have the advantage, though, of being transparent like emerald. As you examine green gems other than emerald, you'll probably discover that there is no gem that can equal a good emerald.

Choosing an engagement ring (or pendant) is an important decision. If you put some thought into it and specify to your jeweler what you want, you should be able to make a selection that you'll enjoy for the rest of your life.

13

Finding a Good Buy

Linda is examining a tray of light-colored tanzanites at a public gem show. Pastel colors look good on her, so she has always been attracted to them. The stones all have the same per-carat price, but show some variation in color and quality. Since Linda has read the *Emerald & Tanzanite Buying Guide*, she is able to recognize quality differences and is aware that the fluorescent lighting is enhancing the blue color in the stones.

She picks out three tanzanites, examines them with a loupe, and has Matthew, the seller, weigh them. Then she asks to see them under a light-bulb or halogen spotlight because she wants a stone that will change from blue to purple under different lights. Matthew helps her select the stone with the most distinct shift of color. By chance, it is also the stone with the best cut. Linda is really happy with the tanzanite and plans to have it set in a pendant which she will help design.

Mel wants to buy his wife an emerald pendant for Christmas. He's read the *Emerald & Tanzanite Buying Guide* and realizes he'll need some expert help. As he shops, he discovers that he knows more about emeralds than a lot of the salespeople.

Eventually he finds a knowledgeable salesperson named Beryl. He tells her he's looking for a pendant with a very fine emerald. It doesn't matter what shape it is as long as it's deep green and relatively clean and transparent. Beryl says she doesn't have any emeralds of that quality mounted in jewelry and suggests he look at some loose ones. She is the first salesperson to invite him to examine the stones under magnification and to point out the negative points along with the good ones. Mel doesn't find a suitable emerald, so Beryl offers to bring in some better emeralds from the store's suppliers. Mel is so impressed with her knowledge and candor that he accepts her offer.

A week later, Mel picks out a $12,000 emerald and Beryl helps him select an attractive mounting for it. An independent gem laboratory issues a very positive appraisal on the stone. Both Mel and his wife are pleased with the pendant. In the future, Mel plans to deal with Beryl for the rest of his jewelry needs.

Shopping for emeralds and tanzanites turned out to be a positive experience for Mel and Linda. This was largely because they took the time to learn about these stones beforehand and/or they dealt with a competent salesperson. Listed below are some guidelines that helped them and can help you.

♦ **Note if the salesperson talks about quality.** Salespeople who only promote their price and their styles may not have quality merchandise and probably will not help you select a stone of acceptable quality. A stone does not have to be of top quality to be acceptable, but it should meet your needs in terms of durability and beauty.

♦ **When judging prices, try to compare stones of the same shape, size, color, clarity, transparency, and cut quality.** All of these factors affect the cost of emerald and tanzanite. Due to the complexity of colored-stone pricing, it's easier for consumers to compare stones that are alike.

♦ **Compare the per-carat prices of stones rather than their total cost.** Otherwise it will be difficult for you to make accurate comparisons. At the wholesale level, gems are priced according to per-carat cost.

♦ **Before buying an emerald or tanzanite, look at a wide range of qualities and types.** This will give you a basis for comparison.

♦ **Be willing to compromise.** As you shop, you may discover that your pocketbook does not match your tastes. You may have to get a stone of a smaller size or lower quality than you would like. Even if your budget is unlimited, you may have to compromise on the size, shape, color, or quality due to lack of availability. Emeralds and tanzanites don't have to be perfect for you to enjoy them.

♦ **Remember that there is no standardized system for grading colored stones.** As a consequence, grades have no meaning other than what the seller or grader assigns to them. This is another reason why you need to look at stones yourself and learn to evaluate quality.

♦ **Note if the salesperson is willing to tell you the bad points about stones along with the good ones.** It's impossible for everything in a jewelry showcase to be wonderful and perfect. Salespeople who care about their customers give them candid, objective information.

◆ **Beware of sales ads that seem too good to be true.** The advertised stones might be of unacceptable quality, or they might be stolen or misrepresented. Jewelers are in business to make money, not to lose it.

◆ **If possible, establish a relationship with a jeweler you can trust and who looks after your interests.** He can help you find buys you wouldn't find on your own.

◆ **Place the emerald or tanzanite on the back of your hand between your fingers and look at it closely**. Then answer the following questions. (A negative answer to any one of the questions suggests the stone may be a poor choice.)

   a. Does most of the stone reflect light and color back to the eye? In other words, does it have "life?"
   b. Does the color of the stone look good next to your skin?
   c. Does the stone look like an emerald or tanzanite? There is no point, for example, in buying a tanzanite that looks like black onyx when you can get real black onyx for much less.

The above guidelines in essence suggest that you learn how to evaluate emeralds and tanzanites. But why is it so important for you to do this? Why should jewelers educate you about gem quality? Is it just to help you compare prices?

No. Learning more about emeralds and tanzanites will help you make a choice you can enjoy for a lifetime and will help you appreciate the unique qualities of the stones you choose. How can you appreciate something you don't understand?

As you learn to examine the color nuances of emeralds, you'll see why they have been prized for so long. If you compare the color of good emeralds to the green colors of nature: grass, trees, plants, etc., you'll see that nothing equals their intensity of color. An awareness of tanzanite's ability to change color and show a mixture of blue, purple, and violet makes you realize how unique it is. As the eminent gemologist George Frederick Kunz has pointed out, these colors have an unusual enduring quality:

> All the fair colors of flowers and foliage, and even the blue of the sky and the glory of the sunset clouds, only last a short time, and are subject to continual change, but the sheen and coloration of precious stones are the same today as they were thousands of years ago and will be for thousands of years to come. In a world of change, this permanence has a charm of its own that was early appreciated. (*The Curious Lore of Precious Stones*, preface, page XV.)

As you examine emeralds for clarity and transparency, your expectations for them will change. Instead of thinking that a good emerald must have a clarity similar to diamond or tanzanite, you will understand how difficult it is to find a deep green emerald that is transparent and eye-clean, and you'll have a greater admiration for top-grade emeralds.

As you learn to examine emeralds and tanzanites for cut, you will appreciate the amount of skill and time required to bring out their beauty. Though nature provides us with the material for gems, man is largely responsible for their brilliance and sparkle.

You don't have to be a millionaire to enjoy emeralds and tanzanites. They come in a range of qualities and colors and sizes. No matter what your budget may be, you'll be able to select better emeralds and tanzanites if you know how to judge their quality. So look at them whenever possible. Take time to analyze them. Ask jewelers to explain their quality differences. Gradually, you'll learn to recognize good value, and you'll see that nothing else can match the beauty and colors of emerald and tanzanite.

Chapter Quizzes

Chapter 4 Quiz (Shape & Cutting Style)

True or False?

1. A 1-ct round emerald would normally cost less than a 1-ct emerald-cut emerald of the same size, color and quality.

2. All step cuts are emerald cuts.

3. Tanzanites are frequently cut into trilliants and cushion shapes.

4. The cabochon cut is usually reserved for "trapiche" and fine-quality emeralds.

5. Brilliant-style cuts have triangular and lozenge shaped facets.

6. A mixed cut normally displays more color than an emerald cut.

Answer the following questions:

7. What is the bottom cone-shaped portion of a stone called?

8. What is the name of the narrow rim around the circumference of a stone?

9. What is the large top facet of a stone called?

Answers:

1. F It would tend to cost more because of its demand and lower yield from the rough.
2. F A step cut with square corners is not an emerald cut, but all emerald cuts are step cuts.
3. T
4. F Most high-quality emerald is faceted today.
5. T
6. F The mixed cut usually displays more brilliance than the emerald cut but not more color.
7. the pavilion
8. the girdle
9. the table

Chapter 5 Quiz (Judging Emerald Color)

True or False?

1. As emeralds get lighter in color, their value decreases.

2. The distinction between green beryl and emerald has been clearly defined by the trade.

3. You should only look at emeralds under a neutral fluorescent light.

4. The more grayish or brownish an emerald is, the less it is worth.

5. Grading emerald color is easier than grading diamond color.

6. The jewelry trade does not have a standardized system for grading colored stones.

7. Emerald and aquamarine have the same chemical composition.

8. Emerald color should be judged against a yellow background.

9. Emeralds that are strongly bluish or yellowish are normally less valued than those which range from slightly bluish to slightly yellowish.

10. An emerald must originate from Colombia to be of good quality.

Answers:

1. T

2. F. There are no clear definitions for emerald or green beryl which have been adopted by the jewelry trade.

3. F. Even though emeralds should be graded under a neutral fluorescent light, when buying them, you should look at them under different kinds of lighting, particularly the types under which they will be worn.

4. T

5. F   Emerald color grading is a lot more complex.

6. T

7. T

8. F   It should be graded against a non-reflective white background.

9. T

10. F   Although most of the finest large emeralds have come from Colombia, high-quality emeralds are also produced in other countries.

Chapter 6 Quiz (Judging Clarity & Transparency)

True or False?

1. Fractures and liquid inclusions are commonly found in emeralds.

2. Fractures are more serious in tanzanite than in emerald.

3. Emeralds and tanzanites don't need to be examined under magnification because what's important is their color and general appearance.

4. Surface cracks are best identified with darkfield or transmitted light.

5. Flaws are less obvious in dark stones than in lighter ones.

6. Emeralds usually have more inclusions than other gems.

7. When evaluating clarity, you should only look at the face-up view of the stone.

8. Most emeralds sold in jewelry are transparent.

9. Darkfield illumination is helpful for detecting internal fractures and fillings.

10. Clarity is the least important factor in determining the price of an emerald.

Answers:

1. T

2. T   Due to tanzanite's cleavage, fractures are more likely to have a detrimental effect on its durability. Also, tanzanite is expected to have a much higher clarity than emerald.

3. F   Cracks which could threaten the durability of the stone may be hard to see with the naked eye. Besides being an aid to clarity grading, magnification is also important for detecting imitations, synthetics and treatments.

4. F   They're best identified with light reflected off the surface of the stone.

5. T

6. T

7. F   You should examine the stones from several different angles.

8. F   Most emeralds found in jewelry range from semi-transparent through semi-translucent.

9. T

10. F   Shape is probably the least important factor. If the clarity is terrible, emeralds and tanzanites will have a low value no matter how good their color is, how well they are cut, or how big they are.

Chapter 7 Quiz (Judging Tanzanite Color)

1. Which would be hardest to match in terms of color?
   a. diamonds
   b. sapphires
   c. tanzanites

2. Under which type of light is tanzanite most likely to look purplish?
   a. fluorescent light
   b. halogen spotlight
   c. daylight

3. Which tanzanite tone would normally be the most highly valued?
   a. medium-light
   b. medium-dark
   c. very dark

4. You're looking at a tanzanite and you see some flashes of red in it. This is because:
   a. you're either tired or you've had too much to drink.
   b. the stone is synthetic.
   c. tanzanite can display colors other than blue, violet, and purple. Stones with red
      highlights are prized by many tanzanite connoisseurs.

True or False?

5. Purple is a more highly valued tanzanite color than blue.

6. Tanzanites which appear to be well matched for color in daylight may not match under halogen spotlights.

7. The less grayish a tanzanite is, the greater its value.

8. It's difficult to find deep blue or purple tanzanites in one-carat sizes.

Answers:

1. c   Tanzanites would be the hardest to match and diamonds would be the easiest.
2. b
3. b   Dark and medium-dark tones tend to be the most valued. Very dark stones with almost no color are generally considered too dark.
4. c
5. F   Blue is normally more highly valued than purple.
6. T
7. T

8. T   It's a lot easier to find tanzanites with a good depth of color in larger sizes.

Chapter 8 Quiz (Judging Cut)

True or False?

1. To insure maximum reflection of light, emeralds must be cut deeper than diamonds.

2. Windowing can reduce the color and brilliance of a gem.

3. The jewelry trade has established formal guidelines on how cut quality should affect price.

4. If a stone is cut too shallow, it will tend to have a "window."

5. Emeralds are usually better proportioned than tanzanite because they cost more.

6. Stones with very thick girdles tend to look large for their weight.

7. Sometimes the poorly cut stones in a parcel are priced the same as those which are well cut.

8. Stones with very thin or uneven girdles may be hard to set.

9. Most emeralds show no windowing.

10. The total cost of a well-cut stone may be about the same as a bulky stone with a lower per-carat price and the same face-up size.

Answers:

1. T

2. T

3. F

4. T

5. F   Since emerald rough is usually more expensive, cutters are more likely to try and save weight at the expense of beauty and symmetry.

6. F   They tend to look small for their weight.

7. T

8. T

9. F   Most emeralds show some windowing, but the degree of windowing varies.

10. T   When you buy bulky stones with bulging pavilions and thick girdles, you end up paying for unnecessary weight which reduces beauty and face-up size.

Chapter 9 Quiz (Treatments)

True or False?

1. Gem treatments allow consumers to have a better selection of stones to choose from.

2. All tanzanite is heat treated.

3. Heat-treated tanzanite will fade if exposed to sunlight.

4. Most emeralds have oil or epoxy fracture fillings.

5. Epoxy fillings tend to last longer than oil fillings.

6. The price of tanzanite is partially based on its color prior to heat treatment.

7. With the aid of a loupe, it's easy for laypeople to detect emerald fractures and fillings.

8. Emeralds are occasionally treated with colored fillers to make them look greener.

9. If an appraiser has a gemologist diploma, then he/she is qualified to appraise emeralds.

10. Appraisals should include relevant treatment information as well as details about the identity, color and quality of a stone.

Answers:

1. T

2. F   Not all of it is treated but the vast majority of it is.

3. F   The color of tanzanite is stable.

4. T

5. T

6. F   It's just the color after heat treatment that counts.

7. F   Even though some fractures and fillings are easy to spot with a loupe, there are others which are hard for trained professionals to detect even with the aid of a microscope. When buying expensive emeralds, professional assistance is essential.

8. T

9. F   Experience, market knowledge, and additional education is required. To obtain a gemologist diploma, you don't need to know how to detect emerald treatments or grade and price emeralds.

10. T

Chapter 10 Quiz (Imitation or Real?)

1. When you look at a green stone through a dichroscope, you see two colors side by side--bluish green and yellowish green. The stone might be:
    a. glass
    b. synthetic emerald
    c. green CZ (cubic zirconia)
    d. none of the above

2. Which is not a characteristic of glass?
    a. gas bubbles
    b. rounded facet edges
    c. dichroism
    d. concave facets

3. Which is not a typical characteristic of emerald?
    a. a reddish or pinkish reaction when viewed through the chelsea filter
    b. a high price tag for high quality
    c. dichroism
    d. a high clarity

True or False?

4. Stones that are sold as emerald triplets are not always composed of emerald.

5. If an emerald has an open-back setting, it is real.

6. A distinguishing characteristic of tanzanite is its strong trichroism.

7. If an emerald is accompanied by a lab report stating it is natural, then it is valuable.

8. Many gem scam victims have bought their gems through the mail or over the phone.

Answers:

1. b Synthetic emerald displays the two same dichroic colors as natural emerald.
2. c
3. d
4. T They are often made of colorless beryl, pale aquamarine, spinel or quartz.
5   F Imitations are also mounted in open back settings.
6. T
7. F If you don't have information about the quality of an emerald, you can't determine its value. Poor quality emeralds are not very valuable.
8. T

Chapter 11 Quiz (Synthetic Emeralds)

1. Which of the following is **not** another name for synthetic emerald?
    a. lab-grown emerald
    b. created emerald
    c. man-made emerald
    d. imitation emerald

2. Synthetic emeralds
    a cost about the same as cubic zirconia
    b. are less durable than natural emeralds
    c. are grown in a laboratory
    d. all of the above

3. Which of the following could help a gemologist distinguish a natural emerald from a synthetic one?
    a. refractive index
    b. high magnification
    c. fluorescence
    d. all of the above

True or False?

4. The inclusions of synthetic emeralds are always very different from those of natural stones.

5. Synthetic emeralds come in a range of qualities.

6. Synthetic emeralds are grown in the same way as cultured pearls.

7. Synthetic emeralds tend to have a higher clarity and transparency than natural emeralds.

8. Gemologists use a combination of tests to determine the identity of gems.

Answers:

1. d
2. c
3. d
4. F
5. T
6. F   Cultured pearls grow in mollusks in natural bodies of water unlike synthetic stones which grow in a laboratory.
7. T
8. T

Chapter 12 Quiz (Caring for your Emerald & Tanzanite Jewelry)

True or False?

1. A good way to clean tanzanite is to wash it in hot soapy water and then rinse it under the cold tap.

2 Emeralds are softer than jade, therefore they are less durable.

3, Tanzanite is susceptible to abrasions.

4. If you don't see any fractures in emerald with a ten power loupe, then it's safe to clean them in an ultrasonic.

5. Emeralds and tanzanites are usually more suitable for necklaces, pins, and earrings than for everyday rings.

6. If a soapy cloth won't clean an emerald, then soak it in some alcohol.

7. Deep green emeralds tend to have fewer fractures than those which are light green.

8. It's advisable to take emerald and tanzanite jewelry off when you get home and relax.

Answers:

1. F   The sudden change of temperature might cause the stone to crack. Clean tanzanites in lukewarm soapy water and rinse with water of the same temperature.

2. F   Although emeralds are less durable than jade, they are harder. Emeralds have a different internal structure and in addition, they often have fractures. Consequently, they are less durable than jade, in spite of their greater hardness. Hardness and durability are not the same.

3. T

4. F   Epoxy fillings are designed to hide cracks. A loupe is not adequate for detecting emerald fillings and fractures. Emeralds should be examined from several angles under a microscope in reflected and darkfield illumination. It's harder to detect fillings in emerald than in diamonds. Laypeople should assume emeralds have fractures and avoid having them cleaned in ultrasonics unless told otherwise by an honest, knowledgeable professional.

5. T   Because everyday rings tend to get constant hard wear.

6, F   Take it to a professional and have it cleaned. Alcohol is a solvent which can dissolve oil fillings.

7. F   Lighter colored emeralds tend to have fewer fractures.

8. T   If you want the jewelry to last. Emeralds and tanzanites cannot withstand the same amount of wear as diamond jewelry.

Appendix

The information below is based mostly on the following sources:

Beryl, by John Sinkankas
Gems, by Robert Webster
GIA Gem Reference Guide
Gems & Gemology: Biron Hydrothermal Synthetic Emerald, by Kane & Liddicoat, Fall 85
                        Russian Flux-grown Synthetic Emeralds, Koivula & Keller, Summer 85
Photoatlas of Inclusions in Gemstones, by Eduard J. Gübelin and John I. Koivula

Chemical, Physical & Optical Characteristics of Emeralds

Chemical composition: $Be_3Al_2(SiO_3)_6$ Beryllium aluminum silicate

Mohs' hardness: Normally 7 1/2 to 8, sometimes less

Specific gravity:

Natural	2.72 (+.18, -.05)	
Chatham	2.645 to 2.665	maybe 2.66
Biron/Kimberley	2.68 to 2.71	
Gilson Type I & II	2.66	
Gilson Type III	2.68-2.69	
Russian flux	2.65 to 2.66	
Hydrothermal	2.67 to 2.71	

Toughness: Poor to good

Cleavage: Indistinct and interrupted basal cleavage

Fracture: Uneven to conchoidal; luster--vitreous to resinous

Streak: White

Crystal system: Hexagonal (trigonal)

Crystal habits: Hexagonal prisms. Crystals are sometimes modified or terminated by pyramids or basal pinacoids.

Optic character:	Doubly refractive, uniaxial negative	
Refractive index:	Natural	1.577-1.583 (±.017)
	Biron/Kimberley	1.569-1.573 (+0.001)
	Chatham	1.561-1.564
	Gilson Type I	1.564-1.569
	Gilson Type II	1.562-1.567
	Gilson Type III (rare)	1.571-1.579
	Linde flux	1.561-1.564
	Russian flux	1.559-1.563
	Hydrothermal	1.566-1.571 to 1.572-1.578
Birefringence:	Natural	.005-.009
	Biron/Kimberley	.004-.005
	Chatham	.003-,004
	Gilson Type I	.005
	Gilson Type II	.005
	Gilson Type III (rare)	.008
	Linde flux	.003
	Russian flux	.004
	Hydrothermal	.005-.006
Dispersion:	.014	
Polish luster:	Vitreous	
Dichroism:	Distinct yellowish-green; bluish-green	
Chelsea-filter reaction:	Natural emerald	Usually pink to red. Most South African and Indian emeralds remain green.
	Chatham	Strong red
	Biron/Kimberley	Strong red
	Linde flux	Dull red or green
	Linde hydrothermal	Strong red
	Russian hydrothermal	Green
Absorption spectra:	Natural emerald	Distinct lines at 683 and 680.5 nm, less distinct lines at 662 and 646, partial absorption between 630 and 580 nm and almost complete absorption of the violet
	Most synthetics	About the same as natural emerald
	Gilson Type III	Additional line around 427 nm, often poorly defined and seen in certain directions through the crystal

Cause of color:	Chromium, vanadium and/or iron. Most gemologists call emeralds colored by iron green beryl. Fine quality emeralds are usually colored by chromium.	
Ultraviolet fluorescence	Natural emerald	Usually inert, some high-chromium emeralds will fluoresce orangy red to red under LW & SW (LW stronger). Oil in fractures of oiled emerald may fluoresce yellowish green to greenish yellow (LW), weaker to inert (SW).
	Biron/Kimberley	Inert (LW & SW)
	Chatham	Weak to moderate red (LW, SW; LW stronger)
	Gilson Type I & II	Weak to moderate red (LW & SW; LW stronger. Some may fluoresce a weak to moderate yellowish green, yellow or orange (LW & SW).
	Gilson Type III	Inert (LW & SW)
	Linde flux	Inert or dull red to LW & SW
	Linde hydrothermal	Bright red to LW & SW
	Russian Flux	Inert (SW), weak to moderate orangy red (LW)
	Russian hydrothermal	inert (LW & SW)
	Seiko	green (LW)
Reaction to heat:	May cause additional fracturing or complete breakage	
Reaction to chemicals:	Resistant to all acids except hydrofluoric, solvents may dissolve oil	
Stability to light:	Stable except for possible fading in stones treated with green oil	

Typical inclusions in natural emerald:

Austrian:	Actinolite, apatite, biotite mica
Brazilian:	Biotite, dolomite, pyrite crystals, chromite grains, growth tubes
Colombian:	Three-phase inclusions with jagged borders composed of a liquid, a gas bubble, and one or more halite (salt) crystals (all mines); albite, albite feldspar, pyrite (Chivor mines), calcite, brown parisite crystallites (Muzo mines)
Indian:	Two-phase inclusions often parallel to each other, mica
Mozambique:	Two-phase inclusions, biotite crystals
Pakistani:	Growth tubes, fluid inclusions, chromite, dolomite, albite feldspar, wispy "veils" resembling those in flux synthetics. An excellent discussion by Eduard Gübelin and 32 color photos of Pakistani emerald inclusions can be found on pages 76-89 of *Emeralds of Pakistan*.

Sandawana:	Tremolite fibers, mica, garnets with a film of limonite and a yellow halo
Tanzanian:	Biotite mica, orthoclase or quartz crystals, 2- or 3-phase inclusions
South African:	Biotite flakes, molybdenite
USSR (Ural):	Biotite mica, actinolite rods
Zambian:	Limonite-filled tubes, muscovite-mica, tourmaline crystals, hematite platelets, brownish rutile prisms

Typical inclusions in synthetic emeralds:

Biron/Kimberley:	Nail-head spicule inclusions with gas and liquid phases, numerous types of growth features, gold and phenakite crystals, healing fissures with screw-like turns, white particles in the form of comet tails and stringers or simply scattered throughout the stone
Chatham, Gilson, Russian flux:	"Fingerprints" and "veils" of whitish, orangy, or brownish flux, platinum and phenakite crystals, parallel growth planes, 2-phase liquid and gas inclusions
Lechleitner overgrowth:	Net-like pattern of shallow surface cracks, thin formations of phenakite in the overgrowth, color discrepancies between facet surfaces due to repolishing, core may show typical beryl inclusions
Lennix:	Black flux relics with a wreath of tiny recrystallized beryls, ragged flux patterns, small groups of flat phenakite crystallites, circular and spherical shapes, 2-phase inclusions
Linde hydrothermal:	Seed plate with single or multiple two phase inclusions protruding from its surface, nailhead spicules, color zoning, groups of phenakite crystallites
Soviet hydrothermal:	Parallel growth features some of which are labeled as hound's-tooth or chevron patterns, colorless phenakite crystals, 2-phase liquid and gas, veils and fingerprints similar to those in natural emerald.
Seiko:	Dust-like particles, colored growth bands parallel to the table facet, twisted "veils"

Chemical, Physical & Optical Characteristics of Tanzanite

Chemical composition:	$Ca_2Al_3(SiO_4)_3(OH)$ Calcium aluminum hydroxysilicate
Mohs' hardness:	6 to 7
Specific gravity:	3.35 (+.10, -.25)

Toughness:	Fair to poor
Cleavage:	Perfect in one direction
Fracture:	Conchoidal to uneven
Streak:	White
Crystal system:	Orthorhombic
Crystal habits:	Multifaceted prisms
Optic character:	Doubly refractive, biaxial positive
Refractive index:	1.691-1.700 (±.005)
Birefringence:	.008 to .013
Dispersion:	.021
Luster:	Polished surfaces are vitreous. Fracture surfaces are vitreous to dull.
Phenomena:	Change of color from blue or violet to purple
Pleochroism:	Strong blue, purple, and often green or yellow, or sometimes red, orange, or brown.
Absorption spectra:	595, 528, 455 nm
Cause of color:	Vanadium
Ultraviolet fluorescence:	Generally Inert
Reaction to heat:	Fuses under jeweler's torch
Reaction to chemicals:	Attacked by hydrochloric and hydrofluoric acid
Stability to light:	Stable

Bibliography

Books and Booklets

Accredited Gemologists Association. *Gem Scams, The Canadian Connection The Search for Gem Standards.* 1993

Ahrens, Joan & Malloy, Ruth. *Hong Kong Gems & Jewelry.* Hong Kong: Delta Dragon, 1986.

Anderson, B. W. *Gem Testing.* Verplanck, NY: Emerson Books, 1985.

Arem, Joel. *Gems & Jewelry.* New York: Bantam, 1986.

Avery, James. *The Right Jewelry for You.* Austin, Texas: Eakin Press, 1988.

Bauer, Jaroslav & Bouska, Vladimir. *Pierres Precieuses et Pierres Fines.* Paris: Bordas, 1985.

Bauer, Dr. Max. *Precious Stones.* Rutland, Vermont & Tokyo: Charles E. Tuttle, 1969.

Beesley, C. R. *Gemstone Training Manual.* American Gemological Laboratories.

Bingham, Anne. *Buying Jewelry.* New York: McGraw Hill, 1989.

Ciprani, Curzio & Borelli, Alessandro. *Simon & Schuster's Guide to Gems and Precious Stones.* New York: Simon da Schuster, 1986.

Federman, David & Hammid, Tino. *Consumer Guide to Colored Gemstones.* Shawnee Mission, KS: Modern Jeweler, 1989.

Gemological Institute of America. *Gem Reference Guide.* Santa Monica, CA: GIA, 1988.
Gemological Institue of America, *The GIA Diamond Dictionary, Third Edition.* Santa Moica, CA: GIA, 1993.

Geolat, Patti, Van Northrup, C., Federman, David. *The Professional's Guide to Jewelry Insurance Appraising.* Lincolnshire, IL: Vance Publishing Corporation, 1994.

Gubelin, Eduard J. & Koivula, John I. *Photoatlas of Inclusions in Gemstones.* Zurich: ABC Edition, 1986.

Hall, Cally. *Gemstones,* Eyewitness Handbooks. London: Dorling Kindersley, 1994.

Jackson, Carole. *Color Me Beautiful.* New York: Ballantine, 1985.

Jewelers of America. *The Gemstone Enhancement Manual.* New York: Jewelers of America, 1990-94.

Kazmi, Ali and Snee, Lawrence. *Emeralds of Pakistan.* New York: Van Nostrand Reinhold, 1989.

Keller, Peter. *Gemsotones of East Africa.* Phoenix: Geoscience Press Inc., 1992.

King, Dawn. *Did Your Jeweler Tell You?* Oasis, Nevada: King Enterprises, 1990.

Kraus, Edward H. & Slawson, Chester B. *Gems & Gem Minerals.* New York: McGraw-Hill, 1947.

Kunz, George Frederick. *The Curious Lore of Precious Stones.* New York: Bell, 1989.
Kunz, George Frederick. *Gems & Precious Stones of North America.* New York: Dover, 1968.

Liddicoat, Richard T. *Handbook of Gem Identification.* Santa Monica, CA: GIA, 1981.

Marcum, David. *Fine Gems and Jewelry.* Homewood, IL: Dow Jones-Irwin, 1986.

Matlins, Antoinette L. & Bonanno, A. *Gem Identification Made Easy.* South Woodstock, VT: Gemstone Press, 1989.
Matlins, Antoinette L. & Bonanno, A. *Jewelry & Gems: The Buying Guide.* South Woodstock, VT: Gemstone Press, 1987.

Meen, V. B. & Tushingham, A. D. *Crown Jewels of Iran.* Toronto: University of Toronto Press, 1968.

Miguel, Jorge. *Jewelry, How to Create Your Image.* Dallas: Taylor Publishing, 1986.

Miller, Anna M. *Gems and Jewelry Appraising.* New York: Van Nostrand Reinhold Company, 1988.

Mumme, I. A. *The Emerald.* Port Hacking, N.S.W.: Mumme Publications, 1982.

Nassau, Kurt. *Gems Made by Man.* Santa Monica, CA: Gemological Institute of America, 1980.
Nassau, Kurt. *Gemstone Enhancement, Second Edition.* London: Butterworths, 1994.

O'Donoghue, Michael. *Identifying Man-made Gems.* London: N.A.G. Press, 1983.

O'Neil, Paul. *Gemstones.* Alexandria, VA: Time-Life Books, 1983.

Preston, William S. *Guides for the Jewelry Industry.* New York: Jewelers Vigilance Committee, Inc., 1986.

Ramsey, John L. & Ramsey, Laura J. *The Collector/Investor Handbook of Gems.* San Diego: Boa Vista Press, 1985.
Read, Peter G. *Gemmology.* Butterworth Heimenman, 1991,

Rubin, Howard. *Grading & Pricing with GemDialogue.* New York: GemDialogue Marketing Co., 1986.

Sauer, Jules Roger. *Emeralds around the World.* Rio de Janeiro: 1992.

Schumann, Walter. *Gemstones of the World.* New York: Sterling, 1977.

Schwartz, Dietmar. *Esmeraldas, Inclusoes em Gemas.* Ouro Preto, Brazil. Federal University of Ouro Preto, 1987.

Sinkankas, John. *Emerald and other Beryls.* Prescott, AZ: Geoscience Press, 1989.
Sinkankas, John. *Gem Cutting: A Lapidary's Manual.* New York: Van Nostrand Reinhold, 1962.
Sinkankas, John. *Van Nostrand's Standard Catalogue of Gems.* New York: Van Nostrand Reinhold, 1968.

Sinkankas, John and Read, Peter. *Beryl.* London: Butterworths. 1986.
Suwa, Yasukazu. *Gemstones Quality & Value* (English Edition). Gemological Institute of America and Suwa & Son, Inc., 1994.

Ward, Fred. *Emeralds.* Bethesda, Md: Gem Book Publishers, 1993.

Webster, Robert. *Gemmologists' Compendium.* New York: Van Nostrand Reinhold, 1979.
Webster, Robert. *Gems, Fourth Edition.* London: Butterworths, 1983.

Wykoff, Gerald L. *Beyond the Glitter.* Washington DC: Adamas, 1982.

Zucker, Benjamin. *How to Buy & Sell Gems: Everyone's Guide to Rubies, Sapphires, Emeralds & Diamonds.* New York: Times Books, 1979.

Articles

Barot, N. R. & Boehm, E. W. Gem-Quality Green Zoisite. *Gems & Gemology.* Spring, pp. 4-15, 1992.

Bosshart, George. "Emeralds from Colombia (Part 1)," *Journal of Gemmology,* April, pp 355-361, 1991.
Bosshart, George. "Emeralds from Colombia (Part 2)," *Journal of Gemmology,* July, pp 409-425, 1991.
Bosshart, George. "Emeralds from Colombia (Part 3)," *Journal of Gemmology,* October, pp 500-503, 1991.

Chatham, Thomas. "Truth in Appraising." *Cornerstone,* July, pp 42-43, 1990.

Dirlam, Dona; Misiorkowski, Elise; Tozer, Rosemary; Stark, Karen; Bassett, Allen. "Gem Wealth of Tanzania. "Gem Wealth of Tanzania." *Gems & Gemology,* Summer, pp 80-101. 1992.

Graziani, G.; Gübelin, E. & Maurizio, M. The Lennix Synthetic Emerald. *Gems & Gemology*. pp 140-147, 1987.

Hanni, H.A., "Identification of fissure-treated gemstones." *Journal of Gemmology*. October, pp 201-205, 1992.

Jennings, R.; Kammerling, R.; Kovaltchouk, A.; Calderon, G.; El Baz, M.; Koivula, J. Emeralds & Green Beryls of Upper Egypt. *Gems & Gemology*. Summer, pp 100-115, 1993.

Kammerling, R.C.; Koivula, J.I.; Kane, R. E.; Maddison, P; Shigley, J.E; and Fritsch E. "Fracture Filling of Emeralds: Opticon and Traditional 'oils'," *Gems & Gemology*, Summer, pp 70-85, 1991.

Kane, Robert & Liddicoat, Richard. "Biron Hydrothermal Synthetic Emerald." *Gems & Gemology*, Fall, 1985.

Koivula, John & Keller, Peter. Russian Flux-grown, Synthetic Emeralds. *Gems & Gemology*. Summer, pp. 79-85, 1985.

Lee, Tom L. "Gemstone Enhancement...Then And Now.' *Colored Stone*. July/August, pp 23-25, 1990.

Levy, Harry. "Fissure Filling of Gemstones." *Gem & Jewellery News*. June. pp 35-27, 1994.

Marcusson, Cynthia R. "Big News Big Blues Tanzanite Makes its 'Presents' Known." *JQ Maganize*, May/June, 1993.

Martin, Deborah. "Gemstone Durability: Design to Display." *Gems & Gemology*. Summer, pp. 63-77, 1987.

Nassau, Kurt. "Two types of historical traps: on 'Diamond Softening' and the 'Antiquity of Oiling'." *Journal of Gemmology*. July, pp 399-403, 1991.

Nassau, Kurt. "Green Glass made of Mt. St. Helen's Ash?" *Gems & Gemology*. Summer, pp.103-104, 1986.

Penner, Ray. The Separation of Natural from Synthetic Emeralds by Non-Microscopic Methods. *Gemmology Canada*. January. pp 6-10, 1994.

Stockton, Carol. The Separation of Natural from Synthetic Emeralds by Infrared Spectroscopy. *Gems & Gemology*. Summer, pp. 96-99. 1987.

Stockton, Carol. The Chemical Distinction of Natural from Synthetic Emerads. *Gems & Gemology*. Fall, pp. 141-145. 1984.

Themelis, Ted. "Inclusion of the month: Oiling emerald." *Lapidary Journal*. March, p. 19, 1990.

Themelis, Ted. "Oiling emeralds." *AGA Cornerstone*. July, pp. 21-24, 1990

Themelis, Ted & Federman, D. "A jeweler's guide to emerald oiling." *Modern Jeweler*. May, pp. 65-69, 1990.

Weldon, Robert. "Epoxy-Like Resins." *Jeweler's Circular Keystone*. June, pp 176-179 1994.

Periodicals

Auction Market Resource for Gems & Jewelry. P. O. Box 7683 Rego Park, NY. 11374.

Canadian Gemmologist. Toronto: Canadian Gemmological Association.

Colored Stone. Devon, PA: *Lapidary Journal* Inc.

GAA Market Monitor Precious Gem Appraisal/Buying Guide. Pittsburgh, PA: GAA.

Gem. Radnnor, PA: Chilton Publishing Co.

Gems and Gemology. Santa Monica, CA: Gemological Institute of America.

Gem & Jewellery News. London. Gemmological Association and Gem Testing Laboratory of Great Britain.

Gemstone Price Reports. Brussels: Ubige S.P.R.L.

The Guide. Chicago: Gemworld International, Inc.

Lapidary Journal. Devon, PA: *Lapidary Journal* Inc.

Jewelers Circular Keystone. Radnor, PA: Chilton Publishing Co.

Jewelers' Quarterly Magazine. Sonoma, CA.

Journal of Gemmology, London: Gemmological Association and Gem Testing Laboratory of Great Britain.

Michelsen Gemstone Index. Pompano Beach, FL: Gem Spectrum.

Modern Jeweler. Lincolnshire, IL: Vance Publishing Inc.

National Jeweler. New York: Gralla Publications.

Palmieri's GAA Market Monitor. Pittsburgh, PA:

Rock & Gem. Ventura, CA: Miller Magazines, Inc.

Miscellaneous: Courses, notes, and leaflets

Beesley, C. R., notes from his AGA seminar on emerald treatments in Tucson, AZ, 1994.

Gemological Institute of America Appraisal Seminar handbook.

Gemological Institute of America Gem Identification Course.

Gemological Institute of America Colored Stone Grading Course.

Gemological Institute of America Colored Stone Grading Course Charts, 1984 & 1989.

Gemological Institute of America Colored Stones Course. 1980 & 1989 editions.

Gemological Institute of America Jewelry Sales Course.

Jewelers of America. *A Guide to What You Should Know About Colored Gemstones.*

Shire, Maurice. *Discovering Emeralds*

Index

Order Form

To: International Jewelry Publications
P.O. Box 13384
Los Angeles, CA 90013-0384 USA

Please send me:

_____ copies of the **EMERALD & TANZANITE BUYING GUIDE**

_____ copies of the **GOLD JEWELRY BUYING GUIDE**

_____ copies of the **PEARL BUYING GUIDE**

_____ copies of the **RUBY & SAPPHIRE BUYING GUIDE**

Within California $21.60 each (includes sales tax)   _____
All other destinations $19.95 US each

_____ copies of the **DIAMOND RING BUYING GUIDE**

Within California $14.02 each (includes sales tax)   _____
All other destinations $12.95 US each   _____

Postage & Handling for Books

USA: first book $1.75, each additional copy $.75   _____
Canada & foreign - surface mail: first book $2.50, ea. addl. $1.50
Canada & Mexico - airmail: first book $3.75, ea. addl. $2.50
All other foreign destinations - airmail: first book $9.00, ea. addl. $5.00

_____ copies of **DIAMONDS: FASCINATING FACTS**.
Within California $4.28 each (includes sales tax)   _____
All other destinations $3.95 US each   _____

Postage for Diamonds: Fascinating Facts
USA: $0.75 per booklet   _____
Canada & Mexico: $0.80 per booklet   _____
All other foreign destinations: surface mail: $1.25 per booklet _____

Total Amount Enclosed   _____
(Check or money order in USA funds)

Ship to:

Name _____

Address _____

City _____ State or Province _____

Postal or Zip Code _____ Country _____

OTHER PUBLICATIONS BY RENEE NEWMAN

The Pearl Buying Guide

"**An interesting and easy-to-understand guide to buying, evaluating, selecting, and caring for pearls and pearl jewelry.** The opening chapters point out common mistakes made when evaluating or buying pearls...Other chapters focus on evaluating pearl types and shapes, luster, nacre thickness, color, flaws, size, weight, length and make. Additional chapters cite differences in South Sea, black, and freshwater pearls, as well as imitation, natural, and cultured pearls. The closing chapters highlight the proper way to care for pearls as well as creative ways to wear them. The many photographs are valuable in illustrating the characteristics of and differences among pearls. Overall, the guide is useful to all types of readers, from the professional jeweler to the average patron..."
Library Journal

"**An easily read, interesting, and helpful book on pearls**...This book would be a good starting place for a jewellery clerk wanting to improve his or her salesmanship, and would even be a help for a graduate gemmologist seeking a better understanding of what to look for when examining or appraising a pearl necklace."
The Canadian Gemmologist

188 pages, 33 color and 89 black/white photos, 7" by 9", $19.95 US.

The Diamond Ring Buying Guide
How to Spot Value & Avoid Ripoffs

"**Filled with useful information, drawings, pictures, and short quizzes** . . . presents helpful suggestions on detecting diamond imitations, in addition to well-though-out discussions of diamond cutting, and how the various factors can influence value . . . a very readable way for the first-time diamond buyer to get acquainted with the often intimidating subject of purchasing a diamond."

Stephen C. Hofer, President, Colored Diamond Laboratory Services, *Jewelers' Circular Keystone*

151 pages, 85 black & white photos, 7" X 9", $12.95 US

AVAILABLE AT bookstores, jewelry supply stores, the GIA, and through the *Lapidary Journal* Book Club or by mail: See reverse side for order form.

Diamonds: Fascinating Facts

An informative booklet with entertaining facts, poems, and statistics about diamonds.

A novel and appropriate greeting card to include with a diamond gift. It comes with a 6" x 9" white envelope. The inside front cover is designed to allow for a personal message.

Full-color, 16-page, self-cover booklet with six 5" by 7 1/2" photos, $3.95 US.

The Ruby & Sapphire Buying Guide

Shows you:
- ♦ How to choose a good-quality stone
- ♦ How to tell a fake from a real ruby or sapphire
- ♦ How to compare prices and save money
- ♦ How to buy gems abroad

"**Solid, informative and comprehensive** . . . dissects each aspect of ruby and sapphire value in detail and quizzes the reader on key points at the end of each chapter. . . a wealth of grading information . . . *The Ruby & Sapphire Buying Guide* is a definite thumbs-up for both the unskilled and semiskilled buyer and seller. There is something here for everyone."

C. R. Beesley, President, American Gemological Laboratories. *Jewelers' Circular Keystone*

'**Highly recommended** . . . includes a great deal of gemmological as well as commercial information; text photographs are clear and cover many situations for appraisal which have rarely been put forward in gemmology texts before. . . . useful to the gemmology student as well as to the dealer or purchaser of jewelry."

The Journal of Gemmology , a publication of the British Gemmological Association

204 pages, 40 color and 85 black/white photos, 7" by 9", $19.95 US.

The Gold Jewelry Buying Guide

A how-to manual on judging jewelry craftsmanship and testing gold, plus practical information on gold chains, Black Hills gold, gold-coin jewelry, and nugget jewelry.

"**Concise, thorough, and completely readable** for the jewelry neophyte. In chapters such as Manufacturing Methods, Gold Terms & Notation, and Judging the Setting, Newman allows consumers confidence and facility in judgements of quality. Professionals in need of quick reference on jewelry evaluation elements may also profit from the completeness and clarity of this book's organization."

Cornerstone, Journal of the Accredited Gemologists Association

"**This book should be required reading for consumers and jewelers alike!** It offers step-by-step instructions for how to examine and judge the quality of craftsmanship and materials even if you know nothing about jewelry. Packed with close-up photos to demonstrate what is right and what is not, this book clears up all the doubts and misconceptions one might have. If you are thinking of buying, making or selling jewelry as a hobby, as a career or just one time, then this book is a great place to start."

Alan Revere, master goldsmith and director of the Revere Academy of Jewelry Arts

172 pages, 35 color and 97 black/white photos, 7" by 9", $19.95 US.

AVAILABLE AT bookstores, jewelry supply stores, the GIA and the *Lapidary Journal* Book Club, or by mail: See reverse side for order form.

Order Form

To: International Jewelry Publications
P.O. Box 13384
Los Angeles, CA 90013-0384 USA

Please send me:

_____ copies of the **EMERALD & TANZANITE BUYING GUIDE**

_____ copies of the **GOLD JEWELRY BUYING GUIDE**

_____ copies of the **PEARL BUYING GUIDE**

_____ copies of the **RUBY & SAPPHIRE BUYING GUIDE**

Within California $21.60 each (includes sales tax) _____
All other destinations $19.95 US each _____

_____ copies of the **DIAMOND RING BUYING GUIDE**

Within California $14.02 each (includes sales tax) _____
All other destinations $12.95 US each _____

Postage & Handling for Books

USA: first book $1.75, each additional copy $.75 _____
Canada & foreign - surface mail: first book $2.50, ea. addl. $1.50 _____
Canada & Mexico - airmail: first book $3.75, ea. addl. $2.50 _____
All other foreign destinations - airmail: first book $9.00, ea. addl. $5.00 _____

_____ copies of **DIAMONDS: FASCINATING FACTS.**
Within California $4.28 each (includes sales tax) _____
All other destinations $3.95 US each _____

Postage for Diamonds: Fascinating Facts
USA: $0.75 per booklet _____
Canada & Mexico: $0.80 per booklet _____
All other foreign destinations: surface mail: $1.25 per booklet _____

Total Amount Enclosed _____
(Check or money order in USA funds)

Ship to:

Name _____

Address _____

City_____ State or Province _____

Postal or Zip Code _____ Country _____